GCSE English Literature AQA Anthology

# Conflict

## The Study Guide
## Higher Level

This book is a step-by-step guide to becoming an expert on the Anthology part of your GCSE English Literature exam.

It's got everything you need to know — annotated poems, key themes, exam advice and worked essays.

It's ideal for use as a classroom study book or a revision guide.

## What CGP is all about

Our sole aim here at CGP is to produce the highest quality books — carefully written, immaculately presented and dangerously close to being funny.

Then we work our socks off to get them out to you — at the cheapest possible prices.

# CONTENTS

## Section Four — Poetry Techniques

## Section Five — The Poetry Exam

## Section Six — Controlled Assessment

## Section Seven — How to Write an A* Answer

Published by CGP

Editors:
Edward Robinson, Hayley Thompson, Emma Warhurst

Produced with:
Alison Smith, Peter Thomas, Nicola Woodfin

Contributors:
Caroline Bagshaw, Kevin Smith, Nicola Woodfin

With thanks to Katherine Reed and Emma Willshaw for the proofreading
and Jan Greenway for copyright research.

ISBN: 978 1 84762 487 1

Clipart from Corel®
Printed by Elanders Ltd, Newcastle upon Tyne.

Based on the classic CGP style created by Richard Parsons.

# How to Use this Book

This guide is for anyone studying the <u>Conflict</u> cluster of the AQA GCSE English Literature <u>Poetry Anthology</u>. You'll have to either answer an <u>exam question</u> on the poems, or write about them for your <u>controlled assessment</u> — your teacher will tell you which.

## Sections One and Two are About The Poems

There are usually <u>two pages</u> about <u>each poem</u>. This is what the pages look like:

There's a nice picture of <u>the poet</u> and some info about their life.

Important or tricky bits of the poem are <u>highlighted</u> and <u>explained</u>.

Difficult words are defined in the <u>poem dictionary</u>.

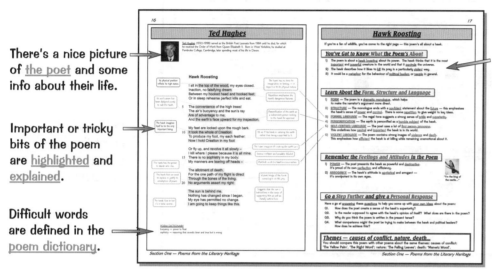

On the right-hand page there are <u>notes</u> about the poem. They include:

- <u>what happens</u> in the poem
- the <u>form</u>, <u>structure</u> and <u>language</u> the poet uses
- the <u>feelings</u> and <u>attitudes</u> in the poem
- a few questions asking you about <u>your feelings</u> on the poem.

If the poem's a bit of a <u>long one</u>, it'll be spread over <u>two pages</u>. One of these will be a <u>pull-out flap</u>. Don't panic. There are full instructions on what to do:

THIS IS A FLAP.
FOLD THIS PAGE OUT.

## It's Really Important You Know Your Stuff

Whether you're doing the exam or the controlled assessment, you need to be really <u>familiar</u> with the poems.

1) You <u>won't notice</u> everything about a poem on <u>first reading</u>. Keep reading these poems over and over and <u>over again</u>.

2) If you notice something about a poem then <u>jot it down</u> — there's <u>no limit</u> to the number of <u>valid points</u> that could be made about these poems.

3) Make sure you have a go at <u>answering</u> those questions at the bottom of the right-hand page.

Nigel's first response to the poems wasn't all that positive.

The questions are designed to make you <u>think for yourself</u> about the poems. You'll get <u>marks</u> in both the exam and the controlled assessment for giving <u>your own ideas</u> and <u>opinions</u> on the texts — it's called a <u>personal response</u>.

# How to Use this Book

You've got to make <u>comparisons</u> between the poems in your writing — so I've included two dead handy sections showing their <u>similarities</u> and <u>differences</u>.  No need to thank me.

## Section Three is About Themes and Ideas

This section will help you make <u>links</u> between the <u>themes</u> presented in the poems — it'll give you loads of <u>ideas</u> of what to write about in your exam or controlled assessment.

A <u>different theme</u> is looked at on <u>each page</u>.

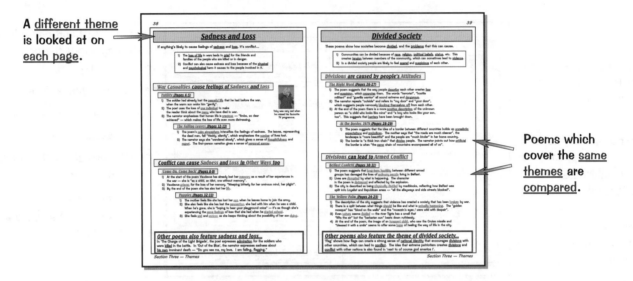

Poems which cover the <u>same</u> <u>themes</u> are <u>compared</u>.

## Section Four is About Poetry Techniques

1)   This section is all about <u>form</u>, <u>structure</u> and <u>language</u>.

2)   It looks at how different poets use features like <u>rhyme</u>, <u>rhythm</u> and <u>imagery</u> to create <u>effects</u> — it's something the examiners are <u>dead keen</u> for you to <u>understand</u> and <u>write about</u>.

Each term is <u>explained</u>...

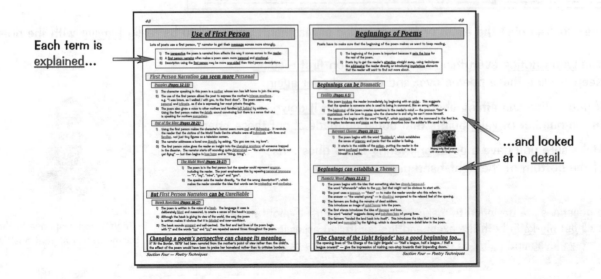

...and looked at in <u>detail</u>.

# How to Use this Book

If you're studying these poems for the <u>Unit 2 exam</u>, then you need <u>Section Five</u>.
If you're doing these poems for your <u>Unit 5 controlled assessment</u>, look at <u>Section Six</u>.

## Section *Five* Tells You What to Do in Your Exam

This is where you can find out <u>exactly</u> what's involved in your <u>Unit 2: Poetry Across Time</u> exam.

There are <u>questions</u> like the ones you'll get in the exam...

... and <u>sample plans</u> to show you different ways to plan your essay.

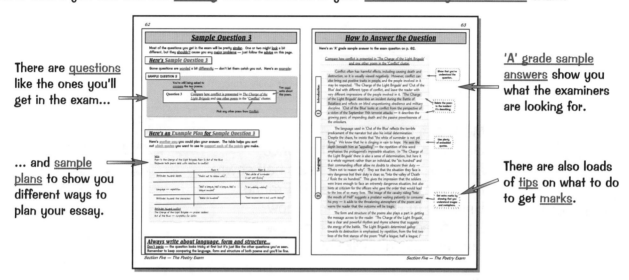

<u>'A' grade sample answers</u> show you what the examiners are looking for.

There are also loads of <u>tips</u> on what to do to get <u>marks</u>.

## Section *Six* Tells You What to Do in Your Controlled Assessment

This section gives you the lowdown on the <u>Unit 5: Exploring Poetry</u> controlled assessment.

There are some <u>example questions</u> like the ones you'll be given, as well as...

...tips on <u>planning</u> and <u>preparing</u> for your assessment piece...

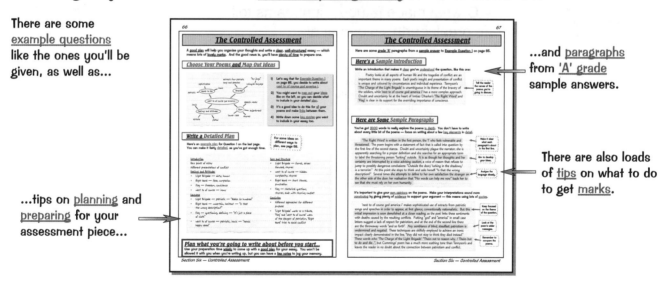

...and <u>paragraphs</u> from <u>'A' grade</u> sample answers.

There are also loads of <u>tips</u> on what to do to get <u>marks</u>.

## Section *Seven* Tells You How to Write An A* Answer

1) Whether you're aiming for an A* or not, this is a really <u>useful</u> section — there are <u>tons of tips</u> for how to <u>improve</u> your work.

2) It tells you how to get the <u>highest marks</u> and gives you <u>loads of examples</u> showing how to do it.

# Wilfred Owen

Wilfred Owen (1893-1918) was born in Shropshire to an English and Welsh family and was best known for his war poems written whilst he served in the trenches in World War One.
He died in battle only one week before the end of the war.

## Futility

> Move him into the sun –
> Gently its touch awoke him once,
> At home, whispering of fields half-sown.
> Always it woke him, even in France,
> 5   Until this morning and this snow.
> If anything might rouse him now
> The kind old sun will know.
>
> Think how it wakes the seeds –
> Woke once the clays of a cold star.
> 10   Are limbs, so dear achieved, are sides,
> Full-nerved, still warm, too hard to stir?
> Was it for this the clay grew tall?
> – O what made fatuous sunbeams toil
> To break earth's sleep at all?

We don't know who he is — he could represent all soldiers damaged by war.

This suggests he can't move himself and makes us wonder why.

Suggests he was a farmer before he had to be a soldier, and also lost potential.

Mentioning France suggests the First World War battlefields.

The sun is personified as a friend.

Both stanzas start with commands — this could be suggesting that the reader must face reality.

This idea is repeated from line 4 to show how important it is — nothing will wake the soldier now. This hints that he's died or that he's alive but incapable of moving himself.

Links with the title — there's a resigned tone.

The sun is powerful and brought the earth to life in the beginning, but it can't help now.

Makes living human beings sound precious — it's hard work to create them.

Questions the reasons for giving life in war — suggests it's pointless.

The poet's anger is coming out — he's hinting at the pointlessness of war.

The questions show the poet's emotion building up. He challenges us to agree or disagree with him.

POEM DICTIONARY
fatuous — unthinkingly foolish

THIS IS A FLAP.
FOLD THIS PAGE OUT.

# Alfred Tennyson

Alfred Tennyson (1809-1892) was born in Lincolnshire and later lived on the Isle of Wight and in Surrey. He studied at Trinity College, Cambridge. Tennyson was one of the great poets of the Victorian era and was Poet Laureate from 1850 to 1892.

## The Charge of the Light Brigade

The rhythm sounds like galloping horses' hooves — it gives the impression that the horses are unstoppable.

Sounds sinister — the reader is warned right from the start that something bad is going to happen.

### 1.
Half a league, half a league,
Half a league onward,
All in the valley of Death
    Rode the six hundred.
5 'Forward, the Light Brigade!
Charge for the guns!' he said:
Into the valley of Death
    Rode the six hundred.

The commanding officer is speaking here.

There's a line in the Bible that says "Though I walk through the valley of the shadow of death, I will fear no evil." (Psalm 23). Using biblical references makes the poem seem solemn and significant.

They're presented as one group with one purpose.

### 2.
'Forward, the Light Brigade!'
10 Was there a man dismay'd?
Not tho' the soldier knew
    Some one had blunder'd:
Theirs not to make reply,
Theirs not to reason why,
15 Theirs but to do and die:
Into the valley of Death
    Rode the six hundred.

Repeating the command from line 5 shows the commanding officer is determined there is no going back.

Soldiers realise the order was a mistake but do what they're told because it's their duty to obey orders. The poet respects them for this.

Rhyme and repetition emphasise the soldiers' obedience and sense of duty, even though they know they will almost certainly be killed.

Repetition makes it clear that they are surrounded by powerful weapons and that there is very little chance of them surviving.

### 3.
Cannon to right of them,
Cannon to left of them,
20 Cannon in front of them
    Volley'd and thunder'd;
Storm'd at with shot and shell,
Boldly they rode and well,
Into the jaws of Death,
25 Into the mouth of Hell
    Rode the six hundred.

Powerful and threatening verbs suggest the noise from the cannons.

Alliteration emphasises the idea of ammunition flying towards them.

The poet admires the soldiers because they are brave and skilful despite the horrors they face.

These images personify death and hell and make them seem like monsters that the soldiers can't escape from.

The first three stanzas end with the same line. It adds to the sense of foreboding and reminds us of the number of soldiers.

# Alfred Tennyson

### 4.

Flash'd all their sabres bare,
Flash'd as they turn'd in air
Sabring the gunners there,
30  Charging an army, while
    All the world wonder'd:
Plunged in the battery-smoke
Right thro' the line they broke;
Cossack and Russian
35  Reel'd from the sabre stroke
    Shatter'd and sunder'd.
Then they rode back, but not
  Not the six hundred.

*This reminds us that the cavalry only had swords against the Russian guns.*

*Could mean that people marvelled at their bravery and also wondered why they had been sent on the charge.*

*The alliteration here sounds vicious.*

*The repetition of "Flash'd" and the rhyme create a powerful image of the cavalry using their swords.*

*They kept going even through a blinding wall of gun smoke — this shows their courage.*

*Although it sounds like they've been successful, it's clear that some of them have been killed.*

### 5.

Cannon to right of them,
40  Cannon to left of them,
Cannon behind them
    Volley'd and thunder'd;
Storm'd at with shot and shell,
While horse and hero fell,
45  They that had fought so well
Came thro' the jaws of Death
Back from the mouth of Hell,
All that was left of them,
  Left of six hundred.

*Similar to the opening lines of stanza 3, but now the soldiers are retreating.*

*The repetition reminds us that lives have been lost, and makes the poem sound sad.*

*The sense of admiration is touched with sadness.*

### 6.

50  When can their glory fade?
O the wild charge they made!
    All the world wonder'd.
Honour the charge they made!
Honour the Light Brigade,
55    Noble six hundred!

*This is a rhetorical question that challenges the reader.*

*Sounds dramatic and daring.*

*Repeated from stanza 4 — it emphasises people's amazement at their bravery.*

*This command is repeated to leave the reader with the idea that they should honour the cavalry.*

*Sums up the way the poet wants the cavalry to be remembered, including the ones who died.*

POEM DICTIONARY
Cossack — a warrior from southern Russia and Ukraine

# Futility

This is quite a depressing poem. But then, with a cluster called "conflict", what did you expect?

## You've Got to Know What the Poem's About

1) The poem is about an <u>injured</u>, probably <u>dead</u>, <u>soldier</u>.
2) It's set in <u>France</u> during the <u>First World War</u>.
3) The poet questions what the <u>point</u> is of <u>life</u> being <u>created</u> if it can be <u>destroyed</u> so easily.

## Learn About the Form, Structure and Language

1) <u>FORM</u> — The poet mainly uses <u>half rhyme</u> (e.g. "seeds" and "sides") rather than full rhyme, which makes the poem seem <u>less formal</u> and more <u>conversational</u>.

2) <u>STRUCTURE</u> — Each stanza begins with a <u>command</u>. The first stanza is a <u>practical</u> instruction about how to help the soldier. In the second stanza the language becomes more <u>philosophical</u> as the poet considers whether creation is worthwhile when life can be ended so quickly.

3) <u>PAST AND PRESENT</u> — The poet uses a mixture of <u>past</u> and <u>present</u> tenses to show the <u>contrast</u> between the soldier's life at home and his current situation. The repeated references to <u>waking</u> emphasise the <u>contrast</u> between being awake and alive and being paralysed or dead.

4) <u>PERSONIFICATION</u> — <u>Nature</u> is personified as <u>powerful</u> but <u>helpless</u> in the face of war.

5) <u>PHILOSOPHICAL LANGUAGE</u> — The language becomes more <u>Biblical</u> and <u>philosophical</u> as the poet reflects on what has happened.

6) <u>DIRECT LANGUAGE</u> — The poet addresses the <u>reader</u> directly, which makes the reader feel more <u>emotionally involved</u> with the poem. The poem contains <u>commands</u> and <u>questions</u> that <u>challenge</u> the reader to think about why the soldier's life has been wasted.

## Remember the Feelings and Attitudes in the Poem

1) <u>SYMPATHY</u> — The poet is <u>sympathetic</u> to the soldier, and uses a <u>kind</u> and <u>respectful</u> tone to talk about him.

2) <u>ANGER AND FRUSTRATION</u> — The poet feels <u>bitter</u> about the <u>waste of life</u> caused by war, and <u>frustrated</u> at the <u>pointlessness</u> of creating life for it to be <u>destroyed</u> by war.

## Go a Step Further and give a Personal Response

Have a go at <u>answering</u> these <u>questions</u> to help you come up with <u>your own ideas</u> about the poem:

Q1.    Is the soldier dead, injured or dying? What clues are there in the poem?

Q2.    How does the title of the poem relate to its content?

Q3.    What can you tell about the poet's attitude to war, and do you agree with it?

## Themes — effects of conflict, sadness and loss, helplessness...

You should compare this poem with other poems about the same themes: sadness and loss: 'The Falling Leaves', 'Come On, Come Back'; effects of conflict: 'Poppies'; helplessness: 'Belfast Confetti'.

THIS IS A FLAP.
FOLD THIS PAGE OUT.

# Stevie Smith

Stevie Smith (1902-1971), real name 'Florence', was born in Kingston upon Hull, but spent most of her life living in North London with her aunt, working for Newnes Publishing Company. She was awarded the Queen's Gold Medal for Poetry in 1969.

## 'Come On, Come Back'

*Incident in a future war*

This is a strong metaphor — when the tide goes out it leaves random objects stranded.

The unusual combination of her being a girl and a soldier is unsettling — it sounds like a contradiction.

Alliteration emphasises the moonlight and creates an eerie setting.

Left by the ebbing tide of battle
On the field of Austerlitz
The girl soldier Vaudevue sits
Her fingers tap the ground, she is alone
5   At midnight in the moonlight she is sitting alone on a round flat stone.

This was a real battleground in the Napoleonic wars.

Repeated for emphasis.

Graded by the Memel Conference first
Of all human exterminators
M.L.5.
Has left her just alive
10  Only her memory is dead for evermore.
She fears and cries, Ah me why am I here?
Sitting alone on a round flat stone on a hummock there.

The imaginary conference on killing suggests how seriously war is still taken in the future.

This is a chilling, clinical, impersonal word.

A disturbing description of how shocked and traumatised she is.

Emphasises Vaudevue's struggle and confusion.

Rising, staggering, over the ground she goes
Over the seeming miles of rutted meadow
15  To the margin of a lake
The sand beneath her feet
Is cold and damp and firm to the waves' beat.

The ground is difficult to walk over — this contrasts with the sand at the end of the stanza.

The physical qualities of the sand contrast with Vaudevue's vagueness.

Quickly – as a child, an idiot, as one without memory –
She strips her uniform off, strips, stands and plunges
20  Into the icy waters of the adorable lake.
On the surface of the water lies
A ribbon of white moonlight
The waters on either side of the moony track
Are black as her mind,
25  Her mind is as secret from her
As the water on which she swims,
As secret as profound as ominous.

Suggests a sudden decision and movement.

This adjective is unexpected — it makes the lake sound innocent and appealing.

A smooth, peaceful image — it sounds tempting.

This sounds unreal and dreamlike.

Emphasises the damage that has been done to Vaudevue — she doesn't know what's happening or what she's doing.

Ending the stanza with this word hints that something bad will happen.

# Stevie Smith

Repeating this word makes the sense of doom stronger.

Weeping bitterly for her ominous mind, her plight,
Up the river of white moonlight she swims
30   Until a treacherous undercurrent
Seizing her in an icy-amorous embrace
Dives with her, swiftly severing
The waters which close above her head.

The oxymoron adds to the eerie atmosphere.

Personification of the undercurrent adds to the surreal atmosphere.

Alliteration emphasises the speed of what is happening. There's a double meaning to "severing" — the undercurrent cuts through the water, and also cuts off Vaudevue's life.

An enemy sentinel
35   Finding the abandoned clothes
Waits for the swimmer's return
('Come on, come back')
Waiting, whiling away the hour
Whittling a shepherd's pipe from the hollow reeds.

Alliteration emphasises the time passing slowly.

This is the title of a song.

A strangely innocent image for a soldier waiting to kill someone.

40   In the chill light of dawn
Ring out the pipe's wild notes
'Come on, come back.'

There are no brackets around the song title this time — it's as if the music's getting louder.

Vaudevue
In the swift and subtle current's close embrace
45   Sleeps on, stirs not, hears not the familiar tune
Favourite of all the troops of all the armies
Favourite of Vaudevue
For she had sung it too
Marching to Austerlitz,
50   'Come on, come back.'

Enemies have some things in common.

It's ironic that Vaudevue sang the same song as her enemy.

Reminds the reader of the beginning of the poem, when Vaudevue had just survived the battle.

The poem ends sadly — Vaudevue won't come back because she's dead.

POEM DICTIONARY
hummock — a little hill
Memel — a real town in Nazi Germany, now in Lithuania
M.L.5. — an imaginary poisonous gas
ominous — suggesting that something bad is going to happen

# The Charge of the Light Brigade

This one's based on a true incident from the Crimean War, where a commanding officer gave an order that led to hundreds of soldiers ending up dead.

## You've Got to Know What the Poem's About

1) The poem describes a disastrous battle between British cavalry (soldiers on horseback) and Russian forces during the Crimean War (1853-1856).

2) A misunderstanding meant that the Light Brigade was ordered to advance into a valley surrounded by enemy soldiers.

3) The cavalry were only armed with swords, whereas the Russian soldiers had guns. The Light Brigade were virtually defenceless against their enemies, and many of them were killed.

## Learn About the Form, Structure and Language

1) FORM — The poem is narrated in the third person, making it seem more like a story. There's a strong, regular, relentless rhythm that creates a fast pace, imitating the cavalry going forward and the energy of the battle.

2) STRUCTURE — The poem tells the story of the battle in chronological order. Some lines and phrases are repeated throughout the poem, sometimes with subtle differences — this keeps the focus on the cavalry troops throughout the poem.

3) REPETITION — Repetition creates a sense of impending doom and the idea that what is going to happen is inevitable. Repetition of "the six hundred" in each stanza reinforces the idea of the large numbers of men involved. It also creates an image of a chaotic battle.

4) VIOLENT LANGUAGE — The poet chooses powerful verbs and adjectives to give a strong sense of the violence of the battle.

5) HEROIC LANGUAGE — The poet uses respectful language to emphasise the soldiers' bravery.

## Remember the Feelings and Attitudes in the Poem

1) ADMIRATION — The poet admires the bravery and sacrifice of the men because they were determined to obey orders even though they knew death was likely. He thinks that the world should recognise their bravery and appreciate their sacrifice.

2) DISBELIEF — The poet seems shocked by the stupidity of the order, but this doesn't diminish his respect for the soldiers who did their duty.

3) HORROR — There's a suggestion that the poet is horrified by the violence of the battle.

## Go a Step Further and give a Personal Response

Have a go at answering these questions to help you come up with your own ideas about the poem:

Q1.    How does the poet show the reader that he has admiration and respect for the cavalry troops?

Q2.    How does the poet convey the sense of how terrifying and violent the battle was?

Q3.    What impression does the poem give of the commanding officers?

## Themes — effects of conflict, reality of battles, patriotism...

You can compare this poem with other poems about the same themes: effects of conflict: 'Poppies', 'Futility'; reality of battles: 'Bayonet Charge'; patriotism: 'next to of course god america i'.

# 'Come On, Come Back'

Another poem about war. This one's set in the future though, which might make it a bit different. Maybe.

## You've Got to Know What the Poem's About

1) The poem starts with a <u>young female soldier</u>, Vaudevue, sitting on the ground. She has just returned from a <u>battle</u> at Austerlitz.

2) Although she has survived, she has been badly <u>injured</u> and has lost her <u>memory</u>, so she's feeling very <u>confused</u> and disturbed.

3) Vaudevue is so <u>distressed</u> that she suddenly strips off and <u>jumps</u> into the <u>lake</u>.

4) An <u>enemy soldier</u> finds Vaudevue's clothes next to the lake and <u>waits</u> for her to come back. Vaudevue <u>doesn't</u> come back though because she is <u>already dead</u>.

## Learn About the Form, Structure and Language

1) <u>FORM</u> — The line lengths are a <u>mixture</u> of short and long, which creates a rambling, <u>conversational</u> feeling, and makes the story seem even more <u>unpredictable</u>. There is some random <u>rhyme</u>, <u>half rhyme</u> and <u>internal rhyme</u> which is sometimes unsettling because it is unexpected. It makes the reader <u>confused</u>, just like Vaudevue.

2) <u>STRUCTURE</u> — The events in the poem are told in <u>chronological order</u>, starting just after Vaudevue fights in the battle at Austerlitz. The last three lines of the poem link back to this battle, creating a <u>circular</u> effect.

3) <u>REPETITION</u> — Repeating the title <u>song</u> reminds the reader of <u>all</u> who have been lost, not just Vaudevue. <u>Key words</u> are also <u>repeated</u> to give the poem a <u>cold</u>, <u>deathly</u> feel.

4) <u>SURREAL LANGUAGE</u> — Strong <u>descriptive images</u> and <u>personification</u> create an <u>eerie</u> atmosphere.

5) <u>PAST AND FUTURE</u> — There are several references to places associated with past wars. The references to <u>war</u> are both <u>historic</u> and <u>futuristic</u>, suggesting that war and its casualties are <u>universal</u> and <u>timeless</u>.

## Remember the Feelings and Attitudes in the Poem

1) <u>IMPERSONAL ATTITUDE</u> — The narrative voice is very <u>impersonal</u>, even though what happens in the poem is very <u>dramatic</u>. The reader might feel <u>sad</u> about Vaudevue's death even though the narrator is <u>detached</u>.

2) <u>IRONY</u> — There's a sense of <u>irony</u> that Vaudevue and her enemy have the <u>same favourite song</u>.

3) <u>MYSTERY</u> — The poem has some mysterious elements like <u>moonlight</u> and <u>pipe music</u>.

## Go a Step Further and give a Personal Response

Have a go at <u>answering</u> these <u>questions</u> to help you come up with <u>your own ideas</u> about the poem:

Q1. What questions does the poem make you want to ask about Vaudevue and the world she lives in?

Q2. How does the poet create a sense of mystery in the poem?

Q3. How is the enemy sentinel depicted in the poem?

Q4. Do you think that the portrayal of the future in this poem is realistic?

## Themes — death, sadness and loss...

You should compare this poem with other poems about the same themes: sadness and loss: 'Futility', 'The Falling Leaves', 'Poppies'; death: 'Out of the Blue', 'Mametz Wood', 'Hawk Roosting'.

# Ted Hughes

Ted Hughes (1930-1998) served as the British Poet Laureate from 1984 until he died, for which he received the Order of Merit from Queen Elizabeth II. Born in West Yorkshire, he studied at Pembroke College, Cambridge, later spending most of his life in Devon.

It sounds like he's in a vulnerable, confused state. It also proves this is real, even though it seems like a nightmare.

He's in uniform — we can picture him as a soldier.

This has a double meaning — it suggests discomfort but also inexperience.

## Bayonet Charge

This shows that he's confused, and that he's facing the gunfire.

Violent imagery describes the sound and impact of the shots.

Contrast between ideals and reality.

Suddenly he awoke and was running – raw
In raw-seamed hot khaki, his sweat heavy,
Stumbling across a field of clods towards a green hedge
That dazzled with rifle fire, hearing
5  Bullets smacking the belly out of the air –
He lugged a rifle numb as a smashed arm;
The patriotic tear that had brimmed in his eye
Sweating like molten iron from the centre of his chest, —

His rifle seems useless.

Suggests that patriotism is irrational.

This stanza pauses the action and focuses on him wondering why he is there.

Emphasises the soldier's insignificance.

It's as if the soldier is turned to stone by his indecision.

In bewilderment then he almost stopped –
10  In what cold clockwork of the stars and the nations
Was he the hand pointing that second?  He was running
Like a man who has jumped up in the dark and runs
Listening between his footfalls for the reason
Of his still running, and his foot hung like
15  Statuary in mid-stride.  Then the shot-slashed furrows

Using an image of someone blind and irrational suggests there's no rational reason for war.

Emphasises frantic movement and suggests confusion.

Suggests pain and fear beyond expression.

He's been reduced to a basic level — he's attacking out of desperation, not moral principle.

Threw up a yellow hare that rolled like a flame
And crawled in a threshing circle, its mouth wide
Open silent, its eyes standing out.
He plunged past with his bayonet toward the green hedge,
20  King, honour, human dignity, etcetera
Dropped like luxuries in a yelling alarm
To get out of that blue crackling air
His terror's touchy dynamite.

A distressing image of out-of-control movement.

These are the reasons that persuade people to go to war.  Using "etcetera" suggests they're not even worth listing.

Natural image contrasts with the violence and terror of war.

Suggests that the soldier's about to lose control of his emotions.

# Bayonet Charge

If you've ever thought that being in a war sounds like fun, this poem might change your mind.

## You've Got to Know What the Poem's About

1) The poem is about a soldier's experience of a <u>violent battle</u>. It describes his thoughts and actions as he desperately tries to <u>avoid</u> being <u>shot</u>.

2) The soldier's overriding emotion and motivation is <u>fear</u>, which has replaced the more <u>patriotic ideals</u> that he held before the violence began.

## Learn About the Form, Structure and Language

1) <u>FORM</u> — The poet uses a lot of <u>enjambment</u> rather than neat line endings. This creates a <u>haphazard</u> effect which represents the soldier's <u>urgency</u> and <u>desperation</u> as he stumbles forward.

2) <u>STRUCTURE</u> — The poem starts in the <u>middle of the action</u> and covers the soldier's movements and thoughts over a short space of time. The middle stanza describes a <u>pause</u> where time seems to briefly <u>stand still</u> and the soldier moves from <u>confusion</u> to <u>terror</u> as the reality of his situation becomes more <u>violent</u>. The final stanza represents a return to <u>panicked movement</u> as he runs for safety.

3) <u>UNIVERSAL LANGUAGE</u> — The poet uses the pronoun "<u>he</u>" rather than naming the soldier to keep him <u>anonymous</u>. It suggests that he is a <u>universal</u> figure who could represent <u>any</u> young soldier.

4) <u>FIGURATIVE LANGUAGE</u> — The poet uses powerful <u>figurative language</u> to emphasise the <u>horror</u> and <u>physical pain</u> of the battle.

5) <u>VIOLENT LANGUAGE</u> — There is some use of shocking imagery to bring home the sights and sounds of war. This helps to convey the sense of <u>confusion</u> and <u>fear</u> to the reader more strongly.

## Remember the Feelings and Attitudes in the Poem

Not that kind
of terror...

1) <u>TERROR</u> — The poem <u>challenges patriotism</u> and shows how desperate <u>terror</u> becomes the overriding emotion in battle. The soldier is driven forward by <u>fear</u> rather than any other more noble motive.

2) <u>CONFUSION</u> — The soldier is confused because he's <u>physically disorientated</u> by the gunfire, but he's also <u>questioning</u> what he's doing there at all.

## Go a Step Further and give a Personal Response

Have a go at <u>answering</u> these <u>questions</u> to help you come up with <u>your own ideas</u> about the poem:

Q1.    How does the middle stanza differ from the other two stanzas?

Q2.    How does the poet show the soldier changing between the start and the end of the poem?

Q3.    How is natural imagery used in the poem to recreate the horror of the soldier's situation?

Q4.    What does the poem suggest about the poet's attitude to war?

## Themes — effects of conflict, reality of battles, nature...

You should compare this poem with other poems about the same themes: effects of conflict: 'The Charge of the Light Brigade', 'Poppies'; reality of battles: 'Belfast Confetti'; nature: 'Mametz Wood'.

# Margaret Postgate Cole

Dame Margaret Postgate Cole (1893-1980) was an English politician and writer who campaigned against conscription during the First World War. She studied at Cambridge and worked as a teacher whilst writing, before entering politics in 1941.

## The Falling Leaves

*November 1915*

Today, as I rode by,
I saw the brown leaves dropping from their tree
In a still afternoon,
When no wind whirled them whistling to the sky,
5   But thickly, silently,
They fell, like snowflakes wiping out the noon;
And wandered slowly thence
For thinking of a gallant multitude
Which now all withering lay,
10   Slain by no wind of age or pestilence,
But in their beauty strewed
Like snowflakes falling on the Flemish clay.

Sounds spontaneous and shows how fast and directly they fell.

Sounds peaceful, but doesn't fit in with what's happening.

Alliteration emphasises the idea that the leaves are old and it is natural for them to fall.

Emphasises the number of leaves falling — they block out the light from the sun.

Shows she's feeling thoughtful.

She praises the soldiers as well as saying how many there are.

She compares them to dead leaves.

Harsh word contrasts with gentleness of first few lines.

This suggests they were still young when they died.

Not a natural death, with no clear reason — linked to line 4.

Snowflakes melt into nothing, just like leaves fall and soldiers' lives are lost and vanish. This also emphasises the sheer numbers.

Thrown around carelessly as though their lives were not important.

There were three major battles in the Flemish province of Ypres in World War One. This makes it clear that the poet is referring to the war.

POEM DICTIONARY
slain — killed deliberately

# The Falling Leaves

'What's a poem about leaves doing in a book about war poetry?', you might be wondering.
Good question. But things aren't quite as they seem...

## You've Got to Know *What* the Poem's *About*

1) The poem is about <u>autumn leaves</u> falling from the trees.
2) The falling leaves remind the poet of young <u>soldiers</u> being <u>killed</u> in war.

## Learn About the *Form, Structure and Language*

1) <u>FORM</u> — The poem is made up of <u>one stanza</u> which contains only <u>one complex sentence</u>. This represents a moment of <u>intense thought</u>. The lines are all <u>different lengths</u> — this could be to suggest the <u>random</u> way that leaves fall. The regular <u>rhyme scheme</u> helps to create a <u>peaceful</u> atmosphere with <u>gentle</u> sounds.

2) <u>STRUCTURE</u> — The poem hinges around the <u>semi-colon</u> in line 6 — before this the poet is describing the <u>leaves falling</u>, and afterwards she switches to describing <u>soldiers</u> being <u>killed</u>. This creates a <u>comparison</u> between leaves falling for no apparent reason and soldiers <u>dying</u> for <u>no good cause</u>.

3) <u>FORMAL LANGUAGE</u> — The poet uses quite <u>formal</u>, <u>old-fashioned</u> vocabulary to describe a simple scene. This adds <u>dignity</u> and <u>gravity</u> to the comparison with the soldiers' <u>deaths</u>.

4) <u>NATURAL IMAGERY</u> — Falling leaves and dying men are both compared to <u>snowflakes</u>. This highlights the sheer <u>number</u> of men killed, the <u>silence</u> of their deaths and how <u>quickly</u> their lives vanished. There is some <u>alliteration</u> to describe <u>natural</u> details like wind and snow.

## Remember the *Feelings and Attitudes* in the Poem

1) <u>SADNESS</u> — The poem has a <u>calm</u>, <u>reflective</u> tone of sadness as the poet imagines the vast numbers of soldiers <u>killed</u> by war.

2) <u>REGRET</u> — There's a sense of sorrow for the <u>deaths</u> that have happened for <u>no clear reason</u>.

3) <u>RESPECT</u> — The poet shows respect for those who gave their <u>lives</u> in the war.

Margaret loved falling leaves — especially if they had poems on them.

## Go a *Step Further* and give a *Personal Response*

Have a go at <u>answering</u> these <u>questions</u> to help you come up with <u>your own ideas</u> about the poem:

Q1.  How does the poet create an atmosphere of sadness in the poem?
Q2.  What details connect the leaves falling and the soldiers dying? What effect does this create?
Q3.  What is the poet's attitude towards the war, and how does she show this in the poem?

## *Themes — death, sadness and loss...*

You should compare this poem with other poems about the same themes: death: 'Out of the Blue', 'Mametz Wood', 'Come On, Come Back'; sadness and loss: 'Futility', 'Poppies'.

# E E Cummings

<u>Edward Estlin Cummings</u> (1894-1962) was an American poet, born in Massachusetts, who studied at Harvard University and later travelled within Europe and North Africa throughout the 1920s and 1930s.

Shows the speaker knows what he's expected to say. Also links America with God, possibly to please listeners.

Suggests speaker can't be bothered to be specific — makes us doubt his integrity.

Scraps of lines from the patriotic song "My Country 'Tis of Thee".

Very dismissive — undermines his commitment.

From "The Star-Spangled Banner", the US national anthem.

He's speaking so hastily that he's mispronounced "golly".

## next to of course god america i

"next to of course god america i
love you land of the pilgrims' and so forth oh
say can you see by the dawn's early my
country 'tis of centuries come and go
5  and are no more what of it we should worry
in every language even deafanddumb
thy sons acclaim your glorious name by gorry
by jingo by gee by gosh by gum
why talk of beauty what could be more beaut-
10  iful than these heroic happy dead
who rushed like lions to the roaring slaughter
they did not stop to think they died instead
then shall the voice of liberty be mute?"

He spoke.  And drank rapidly a glass of water

An extreme claim — we start to wonder if he's telling the truth.

American slang sounds like nonsense here — maybe he's trying to show that he can relate to ordinary people.

It sounds like he's just contradicted himself.

Sounds like an unrealistic cliché for dead soldiers.

Could be praising them but also makes it sound like they didn't think their actions through properly.

Simile creates a powerful image of battle and death, and may imply that death is inevitable.

Stirring rhetorical question to finish with — sounds good but it's confusing.  Is he encouraging more people to fight?  Does he think he represents the "voice of liberty" speaking for the country?

Could suggest he's nervous or that he has even more garbled words to spout.

# next to of course god america i

Nope, that's not a typo — E E Cummings has just shunned normal punctuation and capitalisation rules. You can do that when you're a famous poet.

## You've Got to Know What the Poem's About

1) The poem is a <u>parody</u> of an American <u>patriotic</u>, <u>pro-war</u> speech.
2) The last line makes it clear that the rest of the poem is spoken by a <u>character</u>, rather than reflecting the poet's <u>own opinions</u>.

## Learn About the Form, Structure and Language

1) <u>FORM</u> — The first 13 lines are a <u>first person dramatic monologue</u> and the final line is in the <u>third person</u>, as if the poem is presenting someone giving a <u>speech</u>. The 14 regular lines may be meant to deliberately mimic a <u>sonnet</u> layout — the <u>serious form</u> is <u>undermined</u> by the content just as the serious political speech is <u>parodied</u> by the poem's words.
2) <u>STRUCTURE</u> — The first 13 lines are all within <u>speech marks</u> — the words are <u>fragments</u> of full sentences with very little <u>punctuation</u>, making the phrases sound confusing and meaningless. The last line is the only one that is close to <u>standard English</u>, describing the speaker as he finishes talking. It makes the rest of the poem sound even more <u>empty</u> and <u>meaningless</u>.
3) <u>PATRIOTIC LANGUAGE</u> — The poem sounds <u>stirring</u> and <u>noble</u>, but only in an <u>ironic</u> way. It's an <u>anti-war</u> poem that makes fun of pro-war patriots. It's full of <u>clichés</u> about <u>heroes</u>, <u>beauty</u> and <u>liberty</u>, lines from patriotic <u>songs</u> and over-the-top American <u>slang</u>.
4) <u>RHETORICAL LANGUAGE</u> — The poet uses <u>clichés</u> and <u>exaggerations</u> as the speaker builds up to an <u>emotive end</u>.

## Remember the Feelings and Attitudes in the Poem

1) <u>SARCASM</u> — The poet seems to be <u>mocking</u> the speaker — none of the points is finished or explained, making the speech seem garbled and <u>insincere</u>.
2) <u>CHALLENGING PATRIOTISM</u> — The poem challenges the popular idea of patriotism and sacrifice as something to be <u>complacent</u> about and proud of by making the speaker use ridiculous <u>clichés</u>.
3) <u>ANTI-WAR SENTIMENTS</u> — The poem also raises serious issues about <u>death</u> in war, the <u>sincerity</u> of politicians and leaders and whether we are too <u>gullible</u>.

Well, that's one way of showing patriotism.

## Go a Step Further and give a Personal Response

Have a go at <u>answering</u> these <u>questions</u> to help you come up with <u>your own ideas</u> about the poem:
Q1. What do you think the poet wants the public to do?
Q2. Are the ideas in this poem still relevant today?
Q3. Why has the poet included extracts from such well-known patriotic songs?

## Themes — causes of conflict, patriotism...

You should compare this poem with other poems about the same themes: causes of conflict: 'Hawk Roosting', 'The Yellow Palm', 'The Right Word'; patriotism: 'The Charge of the Light Brigade', 'Flag'.

# *Ted Hughes*

Ted Hughes (1930-1998) served as the British Poet Laureate from 1984 until he died, for which he received the Order of Merit from Queen Elizabeth II. Born in West Yorkshire, he studied at Pembroke College, Cambridge, later spending most of his life in Devon.

## Hawk Roosting

> I sit in the top of the wood, my eyes closed.
> Inaction, no falsifying dream
> Between my hooked head and hooked feet:
> Or in sleep rehearse perfect kills and eat.
>
> 5  The convenience of the high trees!
> The air's buoyancy and the sun's ray
> Are of advantage to me;
> And the earth's face upward for my inspection.
>
> My feet are locked upon the rough bark.
> 10  It took the whole of Creation
> To produce my foot, my each feather:
> Now I hold Creation in my foot
>
> Or fly up, and revolve it all slowly —
> I kill where I please because it is all mine.
> 15  There is no sophistry in my body:
> My manners are tearing off heads —
>
> The allotment of death.
> For the one path of my flight is direct
> Through the bones of the living.
> 20  No arguments assert my right:
>
> The sun is behind me.
> Nothing has changed since I began.
> My eye has permitted no change.
> I am going to keep things like this.

**Annotations:**

- Its physical position reflects its high status.
- It's as if nature has been designed purely to suit the hawk.
- The hawk imagines itself to be the only important being.
- The hawk has the power to decide who dies.
- The hawk feels no need to explain or justify its assumption of power.
- The hawk likes to feel it's in total control.
- The hawk has no time for imagination or fantasy — it stays true to its physical nature.
- Repetition emphasises the hawk's dangerous features.
- Personification of the earth as a subservient person looking to the hawk for approval.
- It's as if the hawk is carrying the earth rather than being supported by it.
- The hawk imagines it's making the earth turn.
- Seems confident and possibly deluded.
- Reminds us of the hawk's vicious nature.
- Violent image of the hawk swooping in on its prey.
- Suggests that the sun is behind it in the sense of supporting it as well as literally behind it.

POEM DICTIONARY
buoyancy — power to float
sophistry — reasoning that sounds clever and true but is wrong

# Hawk Roosting

If you're a fan of wildlife, you've come to the right page — this poem's all about a hawk.

## You've Got to Know What the Poem's About

1) The poem is about a <u>hawk boasting</u> about its power. The hawk thinks that it is the most <u>important</u> and <u>powerful</u> creature in the world and that it <u>controls</u> the universe.

2) The hawk describes how it likes to <u>kill</u> its prey in a particularly <u>violent</u> way.

3) It could be a <u>metaphor</u> for the behaviour of <u>political leaders</u> or <u>people</u> in general.

## Learn About the Form, Structure and Language

1) <u>FORM</u> — The poem is a <u>dramatic monologue</u>, which helps to make the narrator's argument more direct.

2) <u>STRUCTURE</u> — The monologue ends with a <u>confident</u> statement about the <u>future</u> — this emphasises the hawk's sense of <u>power</u> and <u>control</u>. There is some <u>repetition</u> to give weight to key ideas.

3) <u>FORMAL LANGUAGE</u> — The regal tone suggests a strong sense of <u>pride</u> and <u>superiority</u>.

4) <u>PERSONIFICATION</u> — The earth is personified as a <u>humble subject</u> of the hawk.

5) <u>SELF-CENTRED LANGUAGE</u> — The poet uses a lot of <u>first person pronouns</u>. This underlines how <u>central</u> and <u>important</u> the hawk is in its world.

6) <u>VIOLENT LANGUAGE</u> — The poem contains strong images of <u>violence</u> and <u>death</u>. This emphasises how <u>efficient</u> the hawk is at killing while remaining unemotional about it.

## Remember the Feelings and Attitudes in the Poem

1) <u>POWER</u> — The poet presents the hawk as powerful and <u>destructive</u>. It's proud of its own <u>perfection</u> and efficiency.

2) <u>ARROGANCE</u> — The hawk's attitude is <u>egotistical</u> and arrogant — it's omnipotent in its own eyes.

"I'm the king of the castle..."

## Go a Step Further and give a Personal Response

Have a go at <u>answering</u> these <u>questions</u> to help you come up with <u>your own ideas</u> about the poem:

Q1. How does the poet create a sense of the hawk's superiority?

Q2. Is the reader supposed to agree with the hawk's opinion of itself? What clues are there in the poem?

Q3. Why do you think the poem is written in the present tense?

Q4. What comparisons might the poet be trying to make between the hawk and political leaders? How does he achieve this?

## Themes — causes of conflict, nature, death...

You should compare this poem with other poems about the same themes: causes of conflict: 'The Yellow Palm', 'The Right Word'; nature: 'The Falling Leaves'; death: 'Mametz Wood'.

# John Agard

<u>John Agard</u> was born in Guyana in South America in 1949 and moved to Britain in 1977. He likes to perform his poems, and believes humour is an effective way of challenging people's opinions.

The flag could be anywhere — shows how widespread its power is. Different countries have different flags, but they're all the same really.

### Flag

What's that fluttering in a breeze?
It's just a piece of cloth
that brings a nation to its knees.

Repetition reminds us that there is no reason for a flag to have this power — we are the ones who give it the power. This hints at contempt for the flag.

Suggests respect but also the way the flag can control and ruin whole countries because of patriotic behaviour.

Verbs describe simple movements but we make them powerful. The sense of the flag's power increases as the poem goes on — it starts to seem vaguely sinister.

5    What's that unfurling from a pole?
It's just a piece of cloth
that makes the guts of men grow bold.

What's that rising over a tent?
It's just a piece of cloth
that dares the coward to relent.

Could be injuries of war or bravery — the flag plays on our emotions.

The flag of a country inspires men to fight despite their natural fear.

Enjambment puts the focus on "cloth" — a word with very mundane connotations compared to the power a national flag can have.

10   What's that flying across a field?
It's just a piece of cloth
that will outlive the blood you bleed.

Alliteration emphasises violent reality of war and death.

It's as if the flag is alive and doesn't care how many lives are sacrificed for it.

How can I possess such a cloth?
Just ask for a flag, my friend.
15   Then blind your conscience to the end.

The questioner already respects the flag and wants to use its power.

Challenges the reader by making the commands sound easy, but with a sarcastic tone.

Suggests you have to ignore your moral sense to be patriotic — this is what others have done in the past.

Reveals explicitly what the "piece of cloth" is for the first time.

The last two lines rhyme, which creates a kind of bitter punch-line.

# <u>Flag</u>

Flags are more than just pretty-coloured sheets on poles. Or are they...

## You've Got to Know *What the Poem's* About

What's that fluttering in a breeze...

1) The poem is about the power of a <u>national flag</u>. It's presented as a <u>conversation</u> between a naive questioner and a more <u>sceptical</u> responder.

2) One character asks questions about the flag, and the other character responds, explaining that the flag has the power to make people <u>fight wars</u> and <u>die</u>.

## Learn About the *Form, Structure and Language*

1) <u>FORM</u> — The second lines in each stanza are the shortest each time, creating a <u>blunt</u> and slightly <u>cynical</u> tone. The <u>first</u> and <u>third</u> lines <u>rhyme</u> in all except the last stanza — this links the <u>question</u> and <u>answer</u> and helps to make the last word in each stanza <u>significant</u>.

2) <u>STRUCTURE</u> — In each stanza, the questioner asks about a <u>flag</u> — a national symbol of <u>patriotism</u> — and the voice answering explains the <u>powers</u> a flag can have over people. The final stanza is slightly different — the question changes, and the final answer is the most <u>cynical</u>.

3) <u>REPETITION</u> — The <u>question</u> at the start of the first four stanzas has the same <u>sentence structure</u>. It gives the poet a chance to use a range of verbs about the flag and suggests it can be seen in many places.

4) <u>RHETORICAL LANGUAGE</u> — Powerful commands and sarcastic language <u>involve</u> and <u>challenge</u> the reader. The use of informal questions <u>undermines</u> the supposedly noble ideas a flag inspires.

## Remember the *Feelings and Attitudes* in the Poem

1) <u>CYNICISM</u> — The poet mocks the way people will allow a symbol of <u>nationalism</u> like a flag to have such <u>power</u> over them and inspire whole countries to go to war.

2) <u>CONTEMPT</u> — The poet criticises the way people <u>ignore</u> their sense of <u>right and wrong</u> for the demands of <u>patriotism</u>.

3) <u>WARNING</u> — The poem warns us about letting ourselves be <u>manipulated</u> by empty symbols.

## Go a *Step Further* and give a *Personal Response*

Have a go at <u>answering</u> these <u>questions</u> to help you come up with <u>your own ideas</u> about the poem:

Q1. What kind of image of the flag does the poet portray, and how does he do this?

Q2. Why do you think the questioner wants to know how they can "possess such a cloth"?

Q3. Who do you imagine giving the answers in the poem? What might their experiences have been?

Q4. Do you agree with the poet's attitude towards the flag?

## *Themes — causes of conflict and patriotism...*

You should compare this poem with other poems about the same themes: causes of conflict: 'The Yellow Palm'; patriotism: 'Charge of the Light Brigade', 'next to of course god america i'.

# Simon Armitage

<u>Simon Armitage</u> was born in 1963 in West Yorkshire. As well as poetry, he's also written four stage plays, and writes for TV, film and radio. He now teaches creative writing at Manchester Metropolitan University.

### *Extract from* **Out of the Blue**

Sounds vague and anonymous — alliteration emphasises the distance from the people watching.

Implies the reader is watching the TV coverage of the disaster.

> You have picked me out.
> Through a distant shot of a building burning
> you have noticed now
> that a white cotton shirt is twirling, turning.

Repetition emphasises continuous movement.

Gentle, calm movements are misleading at first.

> 5  In fact I am waving, waving.
> Small in the clouds, but waving, waving.
> Does anyone see
> a soul worth saving?

Suggests he feels people are able but unwilling to help.

He is still expecting someone to help, so the style is still conversational — he doesn't sound desperate yet.

> So when will you come?
> 10  Do you think you are watching, watching
> a man shaking crumbs
> or pegging out washing?

Trivial, ordinary actions contrast with the seriousness of the situation.

Repetition reminds us that nobody is acting to save him.

> I am trying and trying.
> The heat behind me is bullying, driving,
> 15  but the white of surrender is not yet flying.
> I am not at the point of leaving, diving.

Reminds the reader that he has been waving a shirt.

Energetic words contrast with the gentle movement of him waving.

> A bird goes by.
> The depth is appalling. Appalling
> that others like me
> 20  should be wind-milling, wheeling, spiralling, falling.

Usually a peaceful image, but here it emphasises that he's very high up.

Using "depth" instead of "height" shows that he's looking down rather than up.

Strong images of air, sky and out-of-control movement. The long list of verbs emphasises how far they are falling.

> Are your eyes believing,
> believing
> that here in the gills
> I am still breathing.

Suggests a fish gasping for air, and continues the underwater imagery of "depth" from line 18.

> 25  But tiring, tiring.
> Sirens below are wailing, firing.
> My arm is numb and my nerves are sagging.
> Do you see me, my love. I am failing, flagging.

Mournful onomatopoeia.

He was previously waving a flag for help, but now he's losing the will to go on.

Reminds us that he's a real person with people who care about him. He's getting more emotional as death approaches.

# Out of the Blue

This is an extract from a long poem called "Out of the Blue" that Armitage wrote in 2006 to commemorate the September 11th terrorist attacks.

## You've Got to Know What the Poem's About

1) The poem is narrated by a victim of the World Trade Centre terrorist attacks in New York on September 11th 2001.

2) The victim is describing being in one of the burning buildings. He addresses someone watching the scene on television.

3) He pleads for help, but it's impossible — the only possible outcome is death.

## Learn About the Form, Structure and Language

1) FORM — The form is similar to an elegy — a mournful poem or song, which is often a lament for someone who has died. There is no regular rhythm but the poem is full of rhyme and internal rhyme. This creates a gentle, sad and helpless tone to the poem. In the first three stanzas, enjambment and questions create a conversational tone.

2) STRUCTURE — In the final four stanzas the voice sounds more urgent as the danger gets closer and the speaker's hope of being rescued begins to vanish. His tone and actions become more desperate toward the end of the poem.

3) VERBS — Verbs in the present continuous tense (using "-ing") give us the feeling that the tragedy is happening as we are watching. It makes us feel as helpless as the victim.

4) QUESTIONS — The questions make it seem like the narrator is asking for help and is slightly confused that he is not being rescued.

## Remember the Feelings and Attitudes in the Poem

1) DESPAIR — There is an increasing sense of despair as the narrator begins to get tired of signalling for help that doesn't come and the fire in the building gets closer.

2) HORROR — The narrator is horrified at the situation and the sight of other victims throwing themselves from the building.

3) INSIGNIFICANCE — There is a sense that the narrator is very small and insignificant — too small to be noticed in the huge scale of the tragedy.

## Go a Step Further and give a Personal Response

Have a go at answering these questions to help you come up with your own ideas about the poem:

Q1. Why is it significant that the narrator is waving a white shirt? How does the poet use this image?

Q2. Is there anything about the poem that inspires sympathy in you? What other emotional reactions do you feel?

Q3. How does the poem link with what you know of the media coverage of the attacks?

Q4. What effect does the poet addressing the reader directly have on you?

## Themes — individual experiences, helplessness and death...

You should compare this poem with other poems about the same themes: individual experiences: 'Poppies'; helplessness: 'Belfast Confetti', 'Futility'; death: 'Mametz Wood', 'Come On, Come Back'.

# Owen Sheers

<u>Owen Sheers</u> was born in 1974 in Fiji but grew up in Abergavenny in South Wales. As well as poetry, he has worked in theatre and television, and was Writer in Residence for The Wordsworth Trust in 2004.

## Mametz Wood

For years afterwards the farmers found them –
the wasted young, turning up under their plough blades
as they tended the land back into itself.

5　A chit of bone, the china plate of a shoulder blade,
the relic of a finger, the blown
and broken bird's egg of a skull,

all mimicked now in flint, breaking blue in white
across this field where they were told to walk, not run,
towards the wood and its nesting machine guns.

10　And even now the earth stands sentinel,
reaching back into itself for reminders of what happened
like a wound working a foreign body to the surface of the skin.

This morning, twenty men buried in one long grave,
a broken mosaic of bone linked arm in arm,
15　their skeletons paused mid dance-macabre

in boots that outlasted them,
their socketed heads tilted back at an angle
and their jaws, those that have them, dropped open.

As if the notes they had sung
20　have only now, with this unearthing,
slipped from their absent tongues.

*Annotations:*

- Refers to the decaying bodies, and also the lives that were wasted.
- Image suggests nursing something wounded.
- Suggests something from the past, but also associated with saints.
- It's difficult to tell which fragments are human and which are stone.
- The earth guards their memory by preserving their bones.
- Links with healing process in line 3.
- Shouldn't normally happen — hints at untimely death.
- Reminds us they have decayed.
- Reminds us of their horrific injuries.
- Emphasises the time it took for them to be discovered and remembered.
- A gentle image — contrasts with the horrific descriptions in the previous stanza.
- The earth can recover after being damaged by war, unlike the dead soldiers.
- Natural image emphasises fragility.
- Suggests the soldiers were betrayed by their orders.
- Natural metaphor to describe weapons has a disturbing effect.
- Reminds us that the soldiers were in a foreign country and implies they shouldn't have died there.
- Image of comradeship.
- Pose suggests fear and desperation and is an unnatural, graphic image of death.
- Continues bird imagery.
- Suggests discovering something from the past.
- Suggests they were shouting or their mouths were open in horror.

<u>POEM DICTIONARY</u>
Mametz Wood — a real place in the Somme region of France — the scene of a battle in 1916 where thousands died
dance-macabre — a medieval dance of death

# *Mametz Wood*

If you go down to Mametz Wood today, you might find something quite unpleasant...

## You've Got to Know *What the Poem's About*

1) The poem is about <u>farmers</u> in France in the present finding <u>bones</u> and <u>skeletons</u> in their fields when they plough the land.

2) The skeletons and bones are from <u>soldiers</u> who died during the <u>First World War</u>. The poem switches between describing their <u>death</u> in battle and the grisly <u>discovery</u> of their skeletons in the present.

## Learn About the *Form, Structure and Language*

1) <u>FORM</u> — The poem is written in <u>tercets</u> (3-line stanzas). It's written in the <u>third person</u>, which gives a feeling of <u>distance</u> and <u>detachment</u>. Long sentences and enjambment give a reflective, <u>sad</u> tone.

2) <u>STRUCTURE</u> — The poem builds up <u>chronologically</u> to the present in stanza 5 where the poet describes the <u>most recent</u> find — twenty skeletons. The thoughtful tone and pace <u>don't change</u> and images of the <u>past</u> are there all through the poem.

3) <u>PERSONIFICATION</u> — The <u>earth</u> is personified as someone who needs <u>healing</u> and as someone guarding the soldiers' <u>memory</u>.

4) <u>FIGURATIVE LANGUAGE</u> — The poem contains lots of <u>similes</u> and <u>metaphors</u> to create vivid images of the <u>rural farmland</u> and ghostly glimpses of <u>past</u> events.

5) <u>PAST AND PRESENT</u> — Images of <u>archaeology</u> are mixed with <u>natural</u> images of the <u>present</u> to show how the bodies of the soldiers have become absorbed into the land.

## Remember the *Feelings and Attitudes in the Poem*

1) <u>SADNESS</u> — The <u>mournful</u>, lyrical tone suggests a <u>calm sadness</u> for the deaths of the young soldiers.

2) <u>UNDERSTATED HORROR</u> — The horror of their death feels <u>distant</u> but is <u>implied</u> by small details — even the <u>grotesque</u> images of the linked skeletons are presented in a <u>gentle</u> tone.

3) <u>MEMORY</u> — The poem contains images of <u>nature</u> making sure that the dead soldiers aren't <u>forgotten</u>. There's a strong sense that <u>memory</u> is important and the <u>past</u> shouldn't be forgotten.

## Go a *Step Further and give a Personal Response*

Have a go at <u>answering</u> these <u>questions</u> to help you come up with <u>your own ideas</u> about the poem:

Q1. The discovery of the 20 linked skeletons in a shallow grave is based on a real event. Who do you think buried them and why might they have arranged them this way?

Q2. The poet's tone seems very detached. What clues can you see to the poet's emotions?

Q3. How and why does the poet create a strong impression of a rural landscape?

## Themes — reality of battles, nature and death...

You should compare this poem with other poems about the same themes: reality of battles: 'Charge of the Light Brigade', 'Bayonet Charge'; nature: 'The Falling Leaves'; death: 'Out of the Blue'.

# Robert Minhinnick

Robert Minhinnick is a Welsh poet and author, born in Neath in 1952. He studied at the University of Wales, and has won numerous awards for both his poetry and novels. He helped to establish two Welsh environmental charities and is an environmental campaigner.

## The Yellow Palm

As I made my way down Palestine Street
I watched a funeral pass –
all the women waving lilac stems
around a coffin made of glass
5   and the face of the man who lay within
who had breathed a poison gas.

As I made my way down Palestine Street
I heard the call to prayer
and I stopped at the door of the golden mosque
10  to watch the faithful there
but there was blood on the walls and the muezzin's eyes
were wild with his despair.

As I made my way down Palestine Street
I met two blind beggars
15  And into their hands I pressed my hands
with a hundred black dinars;
and their salutes were those of the Imperial Guard
in the Mother of all Wars.

As I made my way down Palestine Street
20  I smelled the wide Tigris,
the river smell that lifts the air
in a city such as this;
but down on my head fell the barbarian sun
that knows no armistice.

25  As I made my way down Palestine Street
I saw a Cruise missile,
a slow and silver caravan
on its slow and silver mile,
and a beggar child turned up his face
30  and blessed it with a smile.

As I made my way down Palestine Street
under the yellow palms
I saw their branches hung with yellow dates
all sweeter than salaams,
35  and when that same child reached up to touch,
the fruit fell in his arms.

**Annotations:**

- Repetition of this phrase makes him sound slightly separate from everything going on in the street.
- Sense of sight connected with religious events.
- Sounds like a fairy tale — makes the last line more of a shock.
- An ugly image — his face would be contorted and distressing.
- Sense of hearing connected to religion.
- He still sounds detached.
- Contrasts with the beauty of the mosque and introduces link between religion and violence.
- Links to blind beggars in the next stanza — suggests nobody's seeing clearly.
- Saddam Hussein used this expression about the First Gulf War (1990-1991). It sounds historic but actually refers to a modern war using chemical weapons.
- Sense of touch shows his connection with the people he sees.
- Makes the beggars sound more sinister and hints at a violent past.
- Sense of smell makes the river sound alive.
- Personifies the sun as ruthless — even nature can be in conflict.
- Suggestion of war links with next stanza.
- Makes the child sound innocent and vulnerable.
- Repetition emphasises beauty and grace, even though it's a weapon.
- Presents the child as a holy figure, perhaps because he's not at fault for the war.
- Alliteration emphasises positive words.
- Innocent, positive image suggests that human society could be much more simple and kind.

**POEM DICTIONARY**
Palestine Street — a street in the centre of Baghdad
muezzin — someone who calls people to prayer in a mosque
Imperial Guard — troops who guarded Saddam Hussein
Tigris — the river that runs through Baghdad
Salaam — Islamic greeting meaning 'peace'

# The Yellow Palm

This poem's not a great advert for going on holiday to Baghdad — I think I'll stick to Tenerife.

## You've Got to Know *What the Poem's* About

1) The poem describes what the narrator sees as he walks along a main street in Baghdad.

2) Some of the scenes the narrator sees as he walks along the street are violent or distressing, while others are peaceful and positive.

## Learn About the *Form, Structure and Language*

1) FORM — The poem is a first person ballad. The 2nd, 4th and last lines in each stanza rhyme. Extending the rhyme lets the last two lines act as a kind of comment on the previous description. They introduce extra details that challenge or contradict the images in the previous four lines.

2) STRUCTURE — Each stanza is linked to the next through small associations. This emphasises the idea of a long street full of different but connected things.

3) REPETITION — Repeating the same first line in each stanza emphasises the narrator's movement along the street.

4) VIVID DESCRIPTION — There is a lot of strong imagery and description in the poem. The range of colours makes the description vivid and suggests natural beauty as a background for human violence and distress.

5) SENSES — A range of first person verbs shows the narrator using all his senses — this makes the street feel real and vibrant.

## Remember the *Feelings and Attitudes* in the Poem

1) IMPLIED CRITICISM — The narrator is observing and leaves the reader to make connections between what he sees and moral and political ideas. The poem implies human activity seems aggressive and damaging compared to nature.

2) CONFUSION — The narrator finds contradictions between the innocence and beauty of some of the things he sees and the violence and pain that human society has caused.

3) DETACHMENT — The narrator sounds detached, as though he's presenting us with evidence and letting us draw our own conclusions.

## Go a Step Further *and give a Personal Response*

Have a go at answering these questions to help you come up with your own ideas about the poem:

Q1. The poem is set in Iraq. How is it relevant to other parts of the world?

Q2. Why do you think the poet has made the final stanza the only one without any negative details in it?

Q3. What sort of attitude does the narrator have towards what he sees?

## Themes — causes of conflict and divided society...

You should compare this poem with other poems about the same themes: causes of conflict: 'Hawk Roosting', 'next to of course god america i'; division: 'The Right Word', 'At the Border, 1979'.

# Imtiaz Dharker

Imtiaz Dharker was born in 1954 in Pakistan. She has said that she believes identity comes from "beliefs and states of mind", rather than nationality or religion.

## The Right Word

Outside the door,
lurking in the shadows,
is a terrorist.

*Blunt, emotive choice of noun makes first stanza seem threatening.*

*Two different words for the same action, but one sounds sinister and the other sounds vulnerable.*

Is that the wrong description?
5  Outside that door,
taking shelter in the shadows,
is a freedom-fighter.

*Shows how difficult it is to agree on right and wrong.*

*Sounds noble and idealistic — contrast with stanza 1.*

*Ironic tone suggests there's no right or wrong answer.*

I haven't got this right.
Outside, waiting in the shadows,
10  is a hostile militant.

*Repeated image suggests threat of the unknown and vagueness about what is reality.*

*Repetition reminds reader that extremists often feel like outsiders, excluded from society.*

Are words no more
than waving, wavering flags?
Outside your door,
watchful in the shadows,
15  is a guerrilla warrior.

*Another threatening term suggesting skill, power and violence.*

*An attempt to communicate, but could suggest that patriotism can be misleading. "Wavering" reinforces the idea of uncertainty.*

God help me.
Outside, defying every shadow,
stands a martyr.
I saw his face.

*Frightening idea of someone willing to die and kill for their religious beliefs.*

20  No words can help me now.
Just outside the door,
lost in shadows,
is a child who looks like mine.

*Speaker has become more and more helpless and insecure up to this point.*

*Emotive description takes away the threat and links the speaker and the activist.*

*The activist is just as unsure and uncertain as the speaker.*

One word for you.
25  Outside my door,
his hand too steady,
his eyes too hard
is a boy who looks like your son, too.

*Reminds reader of the shared responsibility for young people.*

*Tone changes here as though the speaker has given up on finding the right term and wants to talk clearly.*

I open the door.
30  Come in, I say.
Come in and eat with us.

*Symbolic of taking down mental barriers created by language.*

*A universal activity, suggesting friendship and hospitality.*

*Repetition emphasises welcome.*

The child steps in
and carefully, at my door,
takes off his shoes.

*Response is gentle and considerate — this shows how things could be.*

*After all the threatening descriptions, this may be "the right word".*

# The Right Word

Sometimes it can be hard to find the right, erm, you know, the right whatsit...

## You've Got to Know What the Poem's About

1) The poem is about a <u>suspicious</u> and <u>divided</u> community, where different viewpoints lead to <u>violence</u>.
2) The narrator tries to find an accurate way to describe a <u>young activist</u> who at first seems threatening.
3) At the end, the activist seems to be just a <u>harmless child</u>.

## Learn About the Form, Structure and Language

1) <u>FORM</u> — The poem is written in the <u>first person</u>, making it seem personal.
   The stanzas have no regular rhythm or rhyme and are of different lengths — this could reflect the difficulty of finding an <u>agreed</u> way of seeing the situation.
2) <u>STRUCTURE</u> — Each of the first seven stanzas is a separate way of <u>describing</u> the young man. Stanzas 1 to 3 are an <u>ironic</u> 'searching' for the correct description, stanzas 4 to 6 suggest that it is <u>too complicated</u> to find a correct description, and stanzas 7 to 9 describe the real <u>truth</u> of the situation. The speaker's tone <u>relaxes</u> in the last two stanzas once a suitable term is found.
3) <u>REPETITION</u> — Several phrases are <u>repeated</u> with slight <u>changes</u> each time, as if the speaker is going back and <u>re-wording</u> them to try to make them more accurate. The repetition of words like "door" and "shadows" keeps up an atmosphere of <u>suspicion</u> and suggests <u>barriers</u> and uncertainty.
4) <u>CONNOTATIVE LANGUAGE</u> — The poet uses a <u>range</u> of nouns and verbs to describe activists and their behaviour, each with different <u>emotional connotations</u>.
5) <u>CONVERSATIONAL STYLE</u> — Using first and second person pronouns and addressing the reader <u>links</u> the speaker and the reader. There are some <u>questions</u> to show that the speaker is struggling to be definite.

## Remember the Feelings and Attitudes in the Poem

1) <u>IMPORTANCE OF LANGUAGE</u> — There is an idea that language is <u>important</u>, and that words can influence people's <u>attitudes</u> and create <u>fear</u> and <u>suspicion</u>. The poem suggests that <u>labelling</u> something can turn it into a <u>threat</u> when it isn't one.
2) <u>ANXIETY</u> — The descriptions of the activist in the first five stanzas show how <u>afraid</u> and <u>suspicious</u> people can be.
3) <u>DESIRE FOR RECONCILIATION</u> — There is a sense of <u>acceptance</u> at the end when the speaker <u>overcomes prejudices</u> and takes the first positive step towards <u>reconciliation</u>.

Mabel was knitting a hat. No, hang on, Mabel was knitting a head-warming device...

## Go a Step Further and give a Personal Response

Have a go at <u>answering</u> these <u>questions</u> to help you come up with <u>your own ideas</u> about the poem:

Q1. What does the poem's title refer to?
Q2. Does language create barriers amongst people in your own society?
Q3. How could this poem be a comment on the behaviour of the media and the general public?

## Themes — causes of conflict and divided society...

You should compare this poem with other poems about the same themes: causes of conflict: 'The Yellow Palm', 'next to of course god america i'; divided society: 'At the Border, 1979'.

# *Choman Hardi*

Choman Hardi was born in 1974 in Iraqi Kurdistan, but spent from 1975 to 1979 with her family in Iran.  In 1993 she arrived in the UK as a refugee, and went on to study at Oxford, London and Kent Universities.  She has published poetry in both Kurdish and English.

### At the Border, 1979

Suggests control by officials.

There's a sense of urgency and anxiety.

'It is your last check-in point in this country!'
We grabbed a drink –
soon everything would taste different.

They expect everything to be different when they're in a different country.

The land under our feet continued
5   divided by a thick iron chain.

An artificial, man-made division.

My sister put her leg across it.
'Look over here,' she said to us,
'my right leg is in this country
and my left leg in the other.'
10   The border guards told her off.

Shows how insignificant the border is physically.

The response is unthreatening and makes the guards seem silly for caring about something trivial.

The mother's exaggeration suggests patriotic prejudice.

My mother informed me: *We are going home.*
She said that the roads are much cleaner
the landscape is more beautiful
and people are much kinder.

Caesura makes the mother's announcement seem grand and significant.

15   Dozens of families waited in the rain.
'I can inhale home,' somebody said.
Now our mothers were crying.  I was five years old
standing by the check-in point
comparing both sides of the border.

Links with line 4 — natural qualities remain the same and divisions are imposed by people.

The adults' reaction seems dramatic.

Repetition for emphasis.

Sounds calm and logical compared to the adults' behaviour.

20   The autumn soil continued on the other side
with the same colour, the same texture.
It rained on both sides of the chain.

Simple statement of fact — unlike the adults, she's unaffected by emotions.

Shows the family at the mercy of official rules.

We waited while our papers were checked,
our faces thoroughly inspected.
25   Then the chain was removed to let us through.
A man bent down and kissed his muddy homeland.
The same chain of mountains encompassed all of us.

Passive construction keeps the controllers anonymous and powerful.

Makes his reaction seem exaggerated, as the land is nothing special.

Contrasts with the earlier image of "chain" — this is a natural boundary holding different people together.

# At the Border, 1979

Crossing a border can be quite emotional. Especially if you trip over it.

## You've Got to Know What the Poem's About

1) The poem is about someone crossing a <u>border</u> back into their <u>homeland</u> as a child. The family sound <u>helpless</u> and anxious.

2) The <u>adults</u> become very <u>emotional</u> about crossing the border and returning to their homeland. The narrator <u>can't understand</u> why it's so important to them when things look <u>the same</u> on both sides of the border.

They're a cheery lot, those border guards...

## Learn About the Form, Structure and Language

1) <u>FORM</u> — The poem is written in the <u>first person</u>, showing it's a personal memory. The stanzas are of unequal length, which suggests <u>fragments of memories</u> occurring to the character as she pieces together memories of the scene. The use of caesura and enjambment reinforce this impression.

2) <u>STRUCTURE</u> — The beginning of the poem uses a lot of <u>direct speech</u>. The tone becomes more <u>reflective</u> in stanzas 6 and 7 as the poet describes the lack of difference between the two sides of the border.

3) <u>CHILD-LIKE LANGUAGE</u> — The poem is written in a <u>simple</u>, <u>conversational</u> style with no elaborate description or imagery. The short sentences create a sense of a child's memory and make the message — that borders are <u>artificial</u> and unnecessary — seem <u>obvious</u>.

4) <u>DIRECT SPEECH</u> — Natural conversation makes the scene more <u>convincing</u> and <u>real</u>.

5) <u>PASSIVE SENTENCES</u> — Impersonal descriptions emphasise how the families are in the power of the <u>officials</u> who decide on national boundaries.

## Remember the Feelings and Attitudes in the Poem

1) <u>NATIONALISM</u> — There's a sense that people have their feelings and attitudes <u>manipulated</u> by nationalism, and that national boundaries and restrictions have <u>negative</u> effects.

2) <u>CHILD-LIKE VIEW</u> — There's a contrast between the <u>logical</u> perspective of a child and the more <u>complex</u> emotions of adults.

## Go a Step Further and give a Personal Response

Have a go at <u>answering</u> these <u>questions</u> to help you come up with <u>your own ideas</u> about the poem:

Q1. Which attitude do you feel most sympathy for — that of the adults in the poem or that of the children? Why?

Q2. Does the poem give you any ideas about why their homeland is so important to the families?

Q3. What examples of humour can you find in the poem? What effect do they have?

## Themes — divided society and helplessness...

You should compare this poem with other poems about the same themes: divided society: 'The Right Word', 'Belfast Confetti', 'The Yellow Palm'; helplessness: 'Out of the Blue', 'Futility'.

# *Ciaran Carson*

<u>Ciaran Carson</u> was born in Belfast in 1948. After graduating from the Queen's University in Belfast he worked for the Arts Council of Northern Ireland. He became a Professor at Queen's University in 1998, as well as being Director of the Seamus Heaney Centre for Poetry.

> Starts in the middle of the action. Riots were sometimes started to lure the security services to the scene of a bomb.

> An image of celebration is violently subverted to describe debris from terrorist bombs.

> Metaphor gives visual image of bomb as well as sense of alarm.

## Belfast Confetti

Suddenly as the riot squad moved in it was raining exclamation marks,
Nuts, bolts, nails, car-keys. A fount of broken type. And the explosion
5  Itself – an asterisk on the map. This hyphenated line, a burst of rapid fire...
I was trying to complete a sentence in my head, but it kept stuttering,
All the alleyways and side streets blocked with stops and
10  colons.

I know this labyrinth so well – Balaklava, Raglan, Inkerman, Odessa Street –
Why can't I escape? Every move is punctuated. Crimea Street. Dead end again.
15  A Saracen, Kremlin-2 mesh. Makrolon face-shields. Walkie-talkies. What is
My name? Where am I coming from? Where am I going? A fusillade of question-marks.

> Suggests broken metal and the failure of words to describe the scene.

> The shape of an explosion, and the way the security forces might mark it on a map.

> Suggests he's trying to escape, but roadblocks prevent him.

> Reflects the sound of gunfire and the speaker's fear.

> Relates to mythology. Makes the fact that he knows the area seem impressive, but he's still trapped.

> Implies violence and hesitation.

> Implies he's having these questions shouted at him.

> It's as though he's being assaulted by the questions.

> He's surrounded by communication from security forces.

<u>POEM DICTIONARY</u>
Balaklava, Raglan, Inkerman, Odessa Street, Crimea Street — areas and roads in Belfast
Saracen — an army vehicle
Makrolon — a type of plastic

# Belfast Confetti

This poem's set in Northern Ireland during 'The Troubles' — a period when there were lots of terrorist incidents between Catholic nationalists and Protestant unionists.

## You've Got to Know What the Poem's About

1) The narrator is caught up in a <u>bomb incident</u> in Belfast.
2) He describes his attempt to get to <u>safety</u> away from the bomb. Every time he tries to escape, his attempts are <u>thwarted</u> by security forces and confusion.

## Learn About the Form, Structure and Language

1) <u>FORM</u> — Irregular line lengths, incomplete sentences, ellipsis and enjambment all give a <u>fragmented</u> feel to the comments, as if the narrator's being <u>interrupted</u> or can't think clearly. Long lines alternate with lines of just a few words, as if the poet keeps reaching <u>dead ends</u>.

2) <u>STRUCTURE</u> — The poem seems to start in the <u>middle</u> of an incident and there is no clear <u>conclusion</u>. The language changes from <u>past</u> to <u>present</u> tense between the first and second stanza to show that the narrator is <u>unable</u> to escape from the scene or the panic in his head.

Debbie and Phil were hoping for just ordinary, run-of-the-mill confetti.

3) <u>IMAGERY</u> — The poem contains lots of strong imagery and metaphors, which describe <u>violence</u> and <u>language</u> in terms of each other — this suggests they have similar <u>damaging</u> effects. It also hints at a <u>failure to communicate</u>.

4) <u>CHAOTIC LANGUAGE</u> — <u>Questions</u> emphasise the <u>confusion</u> and restrictions the character is experiencing. There are lots of <u>lists</u> that make the speaker seem <u>surrounded</u> and create a sense of noise and <u>chaos</u>.

## Remember the Feelings and Attitudes in the Poem

1) <u>BEING TRAPPED</u> — There is a feeling of being trapped by the <u>physical blockades</u> and also harassed by the <u>language</u> used by the security forces to control who goes where.
2) <u>VIOLENCE</u> — <u>Physical</u> and <u>verbal</u> violence confuse and distress the speaker.
3) <u>FEAR AND CONFUSION</u> — The poem shows the personal <u>emotional reaction</u> to a Belfast bomb incident. These were often reported in an <u>impersonal</u> way in the newspapers.

## Go a Step Further and give a Personal Response

Have a go at <u>answering</u> these <u>questions</u> to help you come up with <u>your own ideas</u> about the poem:

Q1. What does the speaker suggest about himself in the poem?
Q2. Is the poem just about the Belfast troubles, or is it relevant to anywhere else in the world?
Q3. Could the poem have anything to say about the way war is reported?

## Themes — reality of battles, divided society...

You should compare this poem with other poems about the same themes: reality of battles: 'The Charge of the Light Brigade', 'Bayonet Charge'; divided society: 'The Right Word', 'The Yellow Palm'.

32

# *Jane Weir*

Jane Weir was born in Salford in 1963 but currently lives and works in Derbyshire. She spent several years in Belfast in Northern Ireland.

## Poppies

Three days before Armistice Sunday
and poppies had already been placed
on individual war graves.  Before you left,
I pinned one onto your lapel, crimped petals,
5  spasms of paper red, disrupting a blockade
of yellow bias binding around your blazer.

Sellotape bandaged around my hand,
I rounded up as many white cat hairs
as I could, smoothed down your shirt's
10  upturned collar, steeled the softening
of my face.  I wanted to graze my nose
across the tip of your nose, play at
being Eskimos like we did when
you were little.  I resisted the impulse
15  to run my fingers through the gelled
blackthorns of your hair.  All my words
flattened, rolled, turned into felt,

slowly melting.  I was brave, as I walked
with you, to the front door, threw
20  it open, the world overflowing
like a treasure chest.  A split second
and you were away, intoxicated.
After you'd gone I went into your bedroom,
released a song bird from its cage.
25  Later a single dove flew from the pear tree,
and this is where it has led me,
skirting the church yard walls, my stomach busy
making tucks, darts, pleats, hat-less, without
a winter coat or reinforcements of scarf, gloves.

30  On reaching the top of the hill I traced
the inscriptions on the war memorial,
leaned against it like a wishbone.
The dove pulled freely against the sky,
an ornamental stitch.  I listened, hoping to hear
35  your playground voice catching on the wind.

**Annotations:**

An ominous reminder that war kills individuals, so loss is personal.

Makes the reader think of an injured body.

Another image of being wounded.  She is emotionally wounded and he might be wounded in war.

Contrasts with the harsh reality he faces now.

Simile shows the world from the son's perspective — makes it sound exciting and full of precious experiences.

Doves are a symbol of peace but also mourning.

Sewing imagery conveys her nervousness and physical feelings of anxiety.

Strong visual image of something small and beautiful in a vast space represents her son.

Repetition emphasises the parallel between national and personal mourning and remembrance.

Suggests that she feels shut out from her son's life.

Could be a school uniform as well as an army one.

She's still treating him like a child.

Alliteration emphasises she's trying to be brave and not show emotion.

Metaphor suggests he's no longer a child because he's styled his hair.  His prickly hair suggests he's unapproachable.

Sudden movement suggests breaking a boundary.

The son's excitement contrasts with his mother's sadness.

Symbolic of her son leaving.

Battle imagery makes her sound vulnerable.

A reminder of the risks her son faces.

Strong visual image hints at her wish for his safety.

Links leaving to join the army with leaving to go to school.

*Section Two — Contemporary Poems*

# Poppies

Poppies are nice. Being a mother whose son goes off to fight in a war isn't quite so nice.

## You've Got to Know What the Poem's About

1) A mother describes her son leaving home to fight in the army.
2) The poem is about the mother's emotional reaction to her son leaving — she feels sad, lonely and scared for his safety.
3) She describes helping him smarten his uniform ready to leave. After he leaves, she goes to places that remind her of him, desperately trying to find any trace of him.

## Learn About the Form, Structure and Language

1) FORM — There is no regular rhyme or rhythm, which helps to make it sound like someone's thoughts and memories. Long sentences and enjambment give an impression of someone absorbed in their own thoughts and memories.
2) STRUCTURE — The poem starts with her son leaving and then goes on to describe what she did afterwards, but the time frame in the poem is ambiguous. A lot of the images could almost describe a young child going to school for the first time.
3) EMOTIONAL LANGUAGE — There are lots of statements beginning with the first person, which gives us a strong impression of the mother's emotions.
4) METAPHORS — Images of war and bereavement are mixed with domestic imagery. Birds are used as symbols of freedom to describe the son leaving the security of his home for the excitement of the wider world.

## Remember the Feelings and Attitudes in the Poem

1) LOSS — The mother is sad about leaving her son.
2) FEAR — She has feelings of anxiety and fear for her son's safety. The poem focuses on the bravery and restraint of the relatives left behind when young people go to war.
3) FREEDOM — The poem shows the contrasting perspectives between the loss the mother feels and the feelings of freedom and excitement her son experiences.

## Go a Step Further and give a Personal Response

Have a go at answering these questions to help you come up with your own ideas about the poem:
Q1. Is this a poem about war or a poem about families?
Q2. What impression does the poet give you of the mother through the things that she does?
Q3. Do you think the son is still alive? What clues does the poem give you?
Q4. How do you think the title relates to the poem?

## Themes — effects of conflict, sadness and loss...

You should compare this poem with other poems about the same themes: effects of conflict: 'The Charge of the Light Brigade'; sadness and loss: 'Futility', 'The Falling Leaves', 'Come On, Come Back'.

# Conflict — Causes

Conflicts can start off as minor <u>disagreements</u>, but they might end up as <u>wars</u>...

> 1) Conflict is when different people, groups or countries <u>disagree</u> with each other.
> 2) Conflict between <u>groups</u> can lead to mistrust, suspicion and violence. Conflict between <u>countries</u> can lead to wars.
> 3) There are many reasons for conflict, including <u>political</u> and <u>religious</u> differences.

## Conflict can be caused by Difference

### The Yellow Palm (Pages 24-25)

1) Faithful citizens have come to pray at the mosque but there is "<u>blood</u> on the walls" and "<u>despair</u>" in the muezzin's eyes. This implies that <u>religion</u> can be a source of conflict.
2) The reference to the "<u>Imperial Guard</u>" (Saddam Hussein's bodyguards) hints at the ongoing influence of a <u>cruel</u> and <u>ambitious</u> leader.
3) The "Cruise missile" was used by <u>US forces</u> in Iraq. This is a reminder of how <u>foreign powers</u> have invaded and interfered in the life of the country.

### Hawk Roosting (Pages 16-17)

1) The narrator is a hawk — a natural <u>predator</u>. It believes that "the allotment of death" is its right.
2) Although the hawk is supremely <u>confident</u>, it is <u>deluding</u> itself — it thinks that it controls the Earth.
3) <u>Pro-war politicians</u> are known as "hawks", so the poem could be describing how arrogant, <u>powerful</u> individuals can lead a whole nation into conflict.

## Language can encourage conflict

### next to of course god america i (Pages 14-15)

1) The poet shows that <u>language</u> can be <u>misused</u> to encourage people to get involved in conflict.
2) The speaker in the poem uses <u>emotive rhetoric</u> to make his listeners keen to fight. Descriptions of "heroic happy dead" who "rushed like lions to the roaring slaughter" sound energetic and <u>exciting</u> but the words "dead" and "slaughter" sound <u>ominous</u>.
3) The last line makes the speaker sound <u>shifty</u> and nervous. The poet seems <u>cynical</u> about the way this character uses the power of language to <u>mislead</u> people.

### Flag (Pages 18-19)

1) The poem shows that <u>patriotism</u> can cause wars if people are <u>influenced</u> more by that than by their <u>conscience</u>.
2) A flag is really "just a piece of cloth", but when people see it as something <u>significant</u> they are willing to <u>kill</u> and <u>die</u> for it — it "makes the guts of men grow bold".

Conflict can also be caused by telling someone they look silly in their leotard.

## Other poems also feature the causes of conflict...

'The Right Word' shows how using <u>suspicious</u> and frightened <u>language</u> can lead to serious problems such as <u>mistrust</u> and <u>fear</u> within a community, which in turn can lead to <u>conflict</u>.

# Conflict — Effects

No prizes for working out that the effects of conflict <u>aren't</u> likely to be good...

> 1) Conflict can cause <u>death</u> and <u>injury</u> to soldiers and civilians.
> 2) People can be <u>psychologically scarred</u> by their experiences.
> 3) Even people <u>not directly involved</u> in conflict can be affected by it, e.g. the families of soldiers fighting in wars.

## Conflict affects the people who Fight

### Futility (Pages 4-5)

1) The poem focuses on the <u>waste</u> of human life caused by war, using an <u>individual</u> soldier to describe the <u>wider effects</u> of war.
2) The narrator feels <u>helpless</u> because he can't restore the soldier's health.
3) He expresses <u>anger</u> and <u>despair</u> that the energy that went into creating life — "limbs, so dear achieved" — has been wasted.

### The Charge of the Light Brigade (Pages 6-7)

1) The poem focuses on the <u>number</u> of men killed in battle as the result of a single order. There are several mentions of "the six hundred", emphasising <u>how many</u> men there were to start with compared to how many <u>survived</u> — "Then they rode back, but not / Not the six hundred".
2) The poem shows that war can inspire great <u>bravery</u> and sacrifice. The soldiers do their duty even though they know they are going to almost certain <u>death</u>.

### Bayonet Charge (Pages 10-11)

1) The poem explores the effect of the experience of battle on an <u>individual</u> — primarily <u>pain</u> and <u>panic</u>. The soldier is a helpless <u>victim</u>, "running", "Stumbling" and "Sweating".
2) Fighting has also <u>destroyed</u> the <u>patriotic ideals</u> that the soldier had to begin with — "King, honour, human dignity, etcetera / Dropped like luxuries".

## Conflict affects people who are Not Directly Involved in it

### Poppies (Pages 32-33)

1) The poem describes the <u>pain</u> and distress of a mother whose son is going away to <u>fight</u> in a war.
2) She feels as if she has <u>lost</u> him even before he has left — his uniform has a "blockade / of yellow bias binding" <u>separating</u> them.
3) After he leaves, her constant anxiety about her son's safety has <u>physical symptoms</u> — she describes her stomach as "busy / making tucks, darts, pleats".
4) References to "war graves" and "the war memorial" remind us of the <u>danger</u> her son faces.

## Other poems also feature the effects of conflict...

'Out of the Blue' shows the <u>devastating</u> effect of political conflict on one man. In 'Come On, Come Back', Vaudevue is so <u>psychologically damaged</u> by war that she ends up <u>dead</u>.

# Reality of Battles

These poems explain what it's <u>really like</u> to be involved in conflict.

> 1) Some poems are set right in the thick of the <u>action</u>.
> 2) Poets can describe the <u>sights</u> and <u>sounds</u> of the battle to enable us to understand what it's really like to be there.

## The Horror of the battle can be Described Explicitly...

### The Charge of the Light Brigade (Pages 6-7)

1) The <u>chaos</u>, <u>noise</u> and <u>danger</u> of the battle is described vividly. The men are "Storm'd at with shot and shell" and "Plunged into the battery-smoke" of the enemies' cannons.
2) The dangerous and terrifying conditions are <u>emphasised</u> by the description of the battleground as "the <u>jaws of Death</u>" and "the <u>mouth of Hell</u>".

### Bayonet Charge (Pages 10-11)

1) The poem focuses on just <u>one individual's</u> experience of battle. There are vivid descriptions of his <u>thoughts</u> and <u>emotions</u>.
2) There is a strong sense of the soldier's physical <u>pain</u> and <u>fear</u>. He is running "In raw-seamed hot khaki" and "Sweating like molten iron". His reaction to the battle is "yelling alarm" and he is motivated by <u>panic</u> — "His terror's touchy dynamite".
3) The physical descriptions of the battle create a sense of <u>noise</u> and <u>confusion</u>. He can hear "Bullets smacking the belly out of the air" and is running through "shot-slashed furrows". The "blue crackling air" and the hedge that "dazzled with rifle fire" give us a clear picture of the <u>dangers</u> he is facing.

### Belfast Confetti (Pages 30-31)

1) The poem describes a <u>distressed</u> and <u>confused</u> individual caught up in a conflict. The first-person voice gives an insight into the character's <u>thoughts</u>.
2) <u>Metaphors</u> for the character's confused thoughts also refer to physical <u>danger</u>, e.g. "a burst / of rapid fire", "A fusillade of question-marks".
3) The description of the explosion raining "nuts, bolts, nails, car keys" emphasises the physical <u>reality</u> of the bomb.

## ...or it can be Implied

### Mametz Wood (Pages 22-23)

1) The <u>horror</u> of the battle is <u>implied</u> by the details of what is being found many years later. The metaphor of "a broken mosaic of bone" and the image of "their jaws, those that have them, dropped open" show how their bodies were <u>shattered</u> by fighting.
2) The <u>fragility</u> of the soldiers' skeletons is emphasised by <u>metaphors</u> like "the china plate of a shoulder blade" and "broken bird's egg of a skull". This suggests how easily they can be <u>damaged</u> in battles.

## Other poems also feature the reality of battles...

'Futility' is about a soldier <u>dying</u> in France in the First World War. 'Hawk Roosting' contains descriptions of a <u>hawk</u> killing its prey, which could suggest killing and being killed in <u>wars</u>.

# Nature

Natural imagery like animals, trees, fields and plants adds to the meaning of these poems.

> 1) Peaceful natural images can provide a contrast if the poem is describing something horrific like a war.
>
> 2) Natural images can also be used as a metaphor to suggest something else.

## Nature can be a Major Theme in the poem

### Hawk Roosting (Pages 16-17)

1) The poem describes violence in a natural setting. In this case, a natural predator is responsible for death, although this may be a metaphor for human violence.

2) The hawk has a controlling relationship with nature, or believes that it does — it says "I hold Creation in my foot". It sees the earth and all of nature as humble and subservient to it.

### The Falling Leaves (Pages 12-13)

1) The poem compares the falling of old leaves — a natural event — with the deaths of young men in war — something that is not natural. The difference is that the "brown leaves" are old and ready to die, whereas the men are still young and have "their beauty".

2) The dead leaves and dead soldiers are both compared to "snowflakes wiping out the noon". The idea of snowflakes blocking out light makes us think of the darkness of death.

## Some poems have nature as the Background

### Mametz Wood (Pages 22-23)

1) The land where the battles took place is described as having been damaged along with the soldiers killed there. Years after the war, the farmers "tended the land back into itself", as though caring for it. This suggests that the land is being restored to its natural purpose.

2) The earth is personified as patient and watchful. It "stands sentinel" as if it's protecting the memory of the soldiers who died, by constantly revealing more of their remains — "reaching back into itself for reminders of what happened".

3) The soldiers' remains are described using images from nature that emphasise their fragility — e.g. "the blown / and broken bird's egg of a skull".

4) The natural metaphor of "nesting machine guns" to describe the weapons used to kill the soldiers suggests that nature was abused by the man-made war.

### Bayonet Charge (Pages 10-11)

1) The natural setting where the battle takes place is described as if its beauty has been destroyed by human fighting.

2) The poem describes the agony of a hare wounded by the gunfire in vivid and disturbing terms. This creates a parallel between the hare's innocence and agony and that of the soldier.

3) The hare "rolled like a flame" and "crawled in a threshing circle" after being hit by a bullet. This helps us imagine the horrific pain the soldier would feel if he was shot.

## Other poems also feature the theme of nature...

'Out of the Blue' uses some natural images like "here in the gills / I am still breathing" to emphasise the narrator's pain and despair. 'The Yellow Palm' includes natural elements like the river and the "barbarian sun" to create a strong impression of what the city of Baghdad is like.

# Sadness and Loss

If anything's likely to cause feelings of <u>sadness</u> and <u>loss</u>, it's conflict...

> 1) The <u>loss of life</u> in wars leads to <u>grief</u> for the friends and families of the people who are killed or in danger.
>
> 2) Conflict can also cause sadness and loss because of the <u>physical</u> and <u>psychological</u> harm it causes to the people involved in it.

## War Casualties *cause feelings of* Sadness *and* Loss

Toby was very sad when he missed his favourite TV programme.

### Futility (Pages 4-5)

1) The soldier had already lost the <u>peaceful life</u> that he had before the war, when the warm sun woke him "gently".
2) The poet uses the loss of <u>one individual</u> to make the reader think about the <u>many</u> who have died in war.
3) The narrator emphasises that human life is <u>precious</u> — "limbs, so dear achieved" — which makes the loss of life even more distressing.

### The Falling Leaves (Pages 12-13)

1) The poem's <u>calm atmosphere</u> intensifies the feelings of sadness. The leaves, representing the dead men, fall "thickly, silently", which emphasises the <u>number</u> of lives lost.
2) The narrator says she "wandered slowly", which gives a sense of <u>thoughtfulness</u> and <u>regret</u>. The first-person narration creates a feeling of <u>personal sorrow</u>.

## Conflict *can cause* Sadness *and* Loss *in Other Ways too*

### 'Come On, Come Back' (Pages 8-9)

1) At the start of the poem Vaudevue has already lost her <u>memory</u> as a result of her experiences in the war — she is "as a child, an idiot, as one without memory".
2) Vaudevue <u>grieves</u> for the loss of her memory, "Weeping bitterly for her ominous mind, her plight".
3) By the end of the poem she has also lost her <u>life</u>.

### Poppies (Pages 32-33)

1) The mother feels like she has lost her <u>son</u> when he leaves home to join the army.
2) She also feels like she has lost the <u>connection</u> she had with him when he was a child. When he's gone, she is "hoping to hear / your playground voice" — it's as though she's experiencing the <u>same feelings</u> of loss that she had when he <u>started school</u>.
3) She feels <u>sad</u> and <u>anxious</u> as she keeps thinking about the possibility of her son <u>dying</u>.

## Other poems also feature sadness and loss...

In 'The Charge of the Light Brigade', the poet expresses <u>admiration</u> for the soldiers who were <u>killed</u> in the battle. In the extract from 'Out of the Blue', the narrator expresses sadness about <u>his own</u> imminent death — "Do you see me, my love. I am failing, flagging."

# Divided Society

These poems show how societies become <u>divided</u>, and the <u>problems</u> that this can cause.

> 1) Communities can be divided because of <u>race</u>, <u>religion</u>, <u>political beliefs</u>, <u>status</u>, etc. This creates <u>tension</u> between members of the community, which can sometimes lead to <u>violence</u>.
>
> 2) In a divided society people are likely to feel <u>scared</u> and <u>suspicious</u> of each other.

## Divisions are caused by people's Attitudes

### The Right Word (Pages 26-27)

1) The poem suggests that the way people <u>describe</u> each other creates <u>fear</u> and <u>suspicion</u>, which <u>separates</u> them. The words "terrorist", "hostile militant" and "guerrilla warrior" all sound extreme and <u>dangerous</u>.

2) The narrator repeats "outside" and refers to "my door" and "your door", which suggests people nervously <u>blocking themselves off</u> from each other.

3) At the end of the poem there is a more <u>positive description</u> of the unknown person as "a child who looks like mine" and "a boy who looks like your son, too". This suggests that <u>barriers</u> have been brought down.

### At the Border, 1979 (Pages 28-29)

1) The poem suggests that the idea of a border between different countries builds up <u>unrealistic</u> <u>expectations</u> and <u>prejudices</u>. The mother says that "the roads are much cleaner", the landscape is "more beautiful" and the people are "much kinder" in her home country.

2) The border is "a thick iron chain" that <u>divides</u> people. The narrator points out how <u>artificial</u> the border is when "the <u>same</u> chain of mountains encompassed all of us".

## Divisions can lead to Armed Conflict

### Belfast Confetti (Pages 30-31)

1) The poem suggests that <u>long-term hostility</u> between different armed groups has damaged the lives of <u>ordinary people</u> living in Belfast.

2) Lives are <u>disrupted</u> by what is happening. The character in the poem is <u>distressed</u> and affected by the explosion.

3) The city is described as being <u>physically divided</u> by roadblocks, reflecting how Belfast was split into Loyalist and Republican areas — "all the alleyways and side streets blocked".

### The Yellow Palm (Pages 24-25)

1) The description of the city suggests that violence has created a society that has been <u>broken</u> by war.

2) There is a split between what things <u>should</u> be like and what is <u>actually happening</u>. The "golden mosque" has "blood on the walls" and the "muezzin's eyes / were wild with despair".

3) Even <u>nature</u> seems <u>divided</u> — the river Tigris has a smell that "lifts the air" but the "barbarian sun" beats down ruthlessly.

4) At the end of the poem, the image of an <u>innocent child</u>, who saw the Cruise missile and "blessed it with a smile" seems to offer some <u>hope</u> of healing the way of life in the city.

## Other poems also feature the theme of divided society...

'Flag' shows how flags can create a strong sense of <u>national identity</u> that encourages <u>divisions</u> with other countries, which can lead to <u>conflict</u>. The idea that extreme patriotism creates <u>divisions</u> and <u>conflict</u> with other nations is also found in 'next to of course god america i'.

# Patriotism

Patriotism can be a <u>good</u> thing, but it can also cause an awful lot of <u>problems</u>...

> 1) Patriotism is <u>dedication</u> to your <u>country</u>.
> 2) When people feel patriotic, they are willing to do whatever they feel their country <u>requires</u> of them — including going to <u>war</u>.

## Patriotism is sometimes Admired

### The Charge of the Light Brigade (Pages 6-7)

1) The men followed the order to charge <u>without question</u>, even though it was clear to them that it was a <u>mistake</u> and that "some one had blunder'd". The poet emphasises their <u>bravery</u> in doing this with the rhetorical question, "Was there a man dismay'd?".
2) The men are portrayed as obedient and determined to do their <u>duty</u> to their country. This commitment to following orders is treated with <u>respect</u> by the poet.
3) The poet <u>admires</u> the men for doing their patriotic duty and for the sacrifice they made. He calls them the "<u>Noble</u> six hundred" and tells us to "<u>Honour</u> the Light Brigade".

## But patriotism can also be Dangerous

### next to of course god america i (Pages 14-15)

1) The poem focuses on the commanders and politicians who <u>abuse</u> patriotism to create <u>conflict</u> and send people to fight.
2) The speaker appeals to his audience's sense of patriotism by using lines from <u>patriotic songs</u>.
3) "<u>By jingo</u>" could refer to <u>jingoism</u> — an <u>extreme</u> from of patriotism that encourages <u>armed conflict</u>.
4) The speaker <u>romanticises</u> the images of battle, mentioning "heroic happy dead", but "they did not stop to think they died instead" suggests an unintentional <u>warning</u>.

### Flag (Pages 18-19)

1) The poem explores how patriotism, symbolised by a national flag, can be <u>damaging</u>. The flag "brings a nation to its knees", <u>controlling</u> and directing people's behaviour through patriotic ideas.
2) Even though the flag is just "a piece of <u>cloth</u>", it has the power to make men <u>fight</u> for their country — it "makes the guts of men grow bold".
3) The poem makes the flag's power sound <u>sinister</u> — we are told it "will outlive the blood you bleed".
4) The poem also implies that the ideals of patriotism can be <u>abused</u>, and that the flag can <u>corrupt</u> people. The listener is told to "blind your <u>conscience</u> to the end" if he wants to use the power the flag holds.

### 'Come On, Come Back' (Pages 8-9)

1) The poem shows that individuals who are <u>fighting</u> against each other because of their patriotism can actually be very <u>similar</u>.
2) The enemy sentinel's favourite song was sung by Vaudevue too, and is the "Favourite of all the troops of all the armies". This suggests that patriotism creates <u>false divisions</u>.
3) Setting the war in the <u>future</u> implies that people will probably <u>go on dying</u> because of patriotism.

## Other poems also feature the theme of patriotism...

'At the Border, 1979' shows how strongly <u>attached</u> people can feel to their home country. They are so <u>happy</u> to be back that "A man bent down and kissed his muddy homeland".

# Individual Experiences

These poems focus on <u>one person</u>'s experience of conflict, rather than the conflict as a whole.

> 1) Conflicts can involve <u>thousands</u> of people, but everyone
>    involved has their own <u>personal experience</u> of it.
> 2) Poets might choose to focus on an individual's experience because it is
>    easier for us as readers to <u>relate</u> to <u>one person</u> rather than a large group.

## Some individuals are Directly Affected by conflict

### Out of the Blue (Pages 20-21)

1) The poem contrasts what people might be seeing on <u>television</u> —
   "a distant shot of a burning building" — with the perspective of an
   <u>individual</u> trapped in one of the towers who asks "Do you see me, my love."
2) What the <u>public</u> is seeing is <u>different</u> to the experience of the <u>victim</u>. The victim
   is waving for help but sarcastically wonders if the people watching see "a man
   shaking crumbs / or pegging out washing".
3) The narrator <u>loses hope</u> throughout the poem. Halfway through he says "I am
   not at the point of leaving, diving", but by the last line he is "<u>failing, flagging</u>".

### Poppies (Pages 32-33)

1) The poem <u>contrasts</u> the perspectives of the <u>son</u>, who is "intoxicated", and the
   <u>mother</u> who is left behind "skirting the churchyard walls" and longing for news.
2) She <u>hides</u> her distress from her son, saying that she
   "steeled the softening / of my face" until after he had gone.
3) Mentioning Armistice Sunday and the war memorial links her fear and pain at the
   thought of losing her son to the <u>common experiences</u> of all the families of soldiers.

## People who are Less Involved have a more Detached view

### The Right Word (Pages 26-27)

1) The narrator addresses us <u>directly</u> as "you" in order to <u>challenge</u> attitudes that we might have.
2) She keeps choosing different words like "<u>terrorist</u>" and "<u>freedom-fighter</u>" to describe the
   young person, before coming to the conclusion that he's just "<u>a child</u>" — this suggests that
   our perception of reality can be <u>distorted</u> if we feel under threat.
3) The poem shows the character <u>overcoming</u> her anxiety to "<u>open the door</u>".

### At the Border, 1979 (Pages 28-29)

1) The poem is written in the <u>first person</u> but is <u>less emotional</u> than the others.
2) The poem expresses how a <u>child</u> is not emotionally affected by the system of
   national boundaries and borders that has been created by <u>adults</u>.
3) There is no direct explanation of how the narrator is <u>feeling</u>. She just says that she stood
   "comparing both sides of the border" and not seeing any significant <u>difference</u> between them.
4) Her innocent view <u>challenges</u> the idea of national boundaries being important and necessary.

## Other poems also feature individual experiences...

'Come On, Come Back' focuses on <u>Vaudevue</u> and shows how badly she has been affected
<u>personally</u> by her experiences of war. 'Bayonet Charge' is about <u>one soldier's</u> personal experience
of fighting in a battle that probably involves <u>hundreds</u> or <u>thousands</u> of others.

# Death

Death is one of the most popular themes in poetry, especially in poems about conflict...

> 1) Death is an inevitable part of any armed conflict.
>
> 2) Death can be narrated from the point of view of the person who's dying, an outsider or someone who is causing death.

## From the perspective of the Dying Person

### Out of the Blue (Pages 20-21)

1) The narrator gets closer and closer to death as the poem goes on, even though he tries to fight against it — he says "I am trying and trying" and "the white of surrender is not yet flying".

2) The narrator seems horrified at the prospect of death as he sees others throw themselves from the building. He says that "The depth is appalling. Appalling".

3) It becomes obvious that if the narrator doesn't jump he will suffocate or burn to death. The building is on fire — "The heat behind me is bullying, driving".

4) He asks if those watching believe that "here in the gills / I am still breathing", which creates an image of a fish gasping in the air and dying.

### 'Come On, Come Back' (Pages 8-9)

1) Death is presented as something welcome for Vaudevue, because war has been so damaging to her.

2) The lake is described as "adorable", suggesting that it is something positive. When she swims, the current seizes her "in an icy-amorous embrace", as if it's rescuing her from her pain.

## From an Outsider's perspective

### Mametz Wood (Pages 22-23)

1) The references to death in the poem are surrounded by peaceful and reflective images. The deaths happened many years earlier and the remains of the soldiers who died are being found by farmers who are looking after the land.

2) The descriptions of the way the bones are found help us to imagine the horror of their deaths. The poem refers to "their jaws, those that have them" and "their absent tongues" — this reminds us that their bodies have been destroyed by gunfire and by decay.

## From the Killer's perspective

### Hawk Roosting (Pages 16-17)

1) The hawk has a practical, unsentimental approach to the death it deals. The hawk believes it has the right to decide whether other creatures live or die, saying "I kill where I please because it is all mine".

2) There is a sense of pride in its destructive power — it boasts about its "perfect kills", and describes "my hooked head and hooked feet" as if they are perfectly-formed tools. It says that his flight path is "direct / Through the bones of the living".

3) The death the hawk controls sounds violent and vicious but also quick and impersonal — it talks about "tearing off heads".

## Other poems also feature the theme of death...

'Futility' is about the death of a young soldier. 'The Charge of the Light Brigade' deals with the deaths of hundreds of men. In 'The Falling Leaves' the narrator expresses sadness about the huge numbers of deaths caused by wars. The theme of death also features in 'The Yellow Palm'.

# Helplessness

Conflicts can often make the people involved in them feel <u>helpless</u> and <u>powerless</u>.

> 1) People feel <u>helpless</u> when they're in a situation that they <u>can't control</u>.
> 2) Sometimes people are helpless because they are being <u>controlled</u> by other people.
> 3) Situations like wars also make people feel helpless, because there's <u>nothing</u> they can do to stop them.

## Helplessness is caused by Not Being In Control

### At the Border, 1979 (Pages 28-29)

1) The families in the poem are <u>refugees</u> who are being allowed to return to their <u>homeland</u>.
2) They are <u>powerless</u> against the authority of the <u>border guards</u> — they have to wait "while our papers were checked, / our faces thoroughly inspected".

### Belfast Confetti (Pages 30-31)

1) The narrator is struggling to cope with a situation that is <u>beyond his control</u>. The sectarian clashes in Belfast often involved <u>innocent citizens</u> like this character.
2) The narrator is feeling physically <u>trapped</u> and finding it hard to <u>think</u> coherently or express himself in <u>words</u>.
3) He is helpless because, although the city is <u>familiar</u> to him ("I know this labyrinth so well"), it has been <u>taken over</u> by security forces and he is powerless to escape.

## People are Helpless in the face of Death

### Out of the Blue (Pages 20-21)

1) The narrator is presented as someone <u>small</u> and <u>insignificant</u> compared to the huge towers of the World Trade Centre and the <u>massive political significance</u> of the attack. He describes himself as "Small in the clouds" and wonders if anyone will come to <u>help</u> him — "Does anyone see / a soul worth saving?"
2) All he can do is <u>wait</u> for help — he asks "So when will you come?"
3) By the end of the poem he is <u>losing</u> his <u>physical strength</u> ("My arm is numb") and his <u>emotional strength</u> ("my nerves are sagging").

### Futility (Pages 4-5)

1) The <u>title</u> of the poem refers to the <u>uselessness</u> of the attempts to help the soldier. It's clear right from the beginning of the poem that the narrator <u>won't succeed</u>.
2) As a <u>last resort</u>, the narrator suggests moving the soldier into the <u>sun</u> — "If anything might rouse him now / The kind old sun will know". However, even the sun that "wakes the seeds" is <u>helpless</u> in the face of death.
3) The narrator's helplessness makes him <u>angry</u> and his question, "Was it for this the clay grew tall?" suggests that there is <u>no point</u> in creating human life if it's going to end like this.

## Other poems also feature the theme of helplessness...

There's a sense of <u>inevitability</u> and helplessness about the deaths in 'The Charge of the Light Brigade' and 'The Falling Leaves'. The mother in 'Poppies' feels helpless because her son is going into a dangerous situation and there's <u>nothing</u> she can do to <u>protect</u> him.

# Forms of Poetry

Different <u>forms</u> of poetry are traditionally used to write about different <u>subjects</u>...

> 1)  The form and structure a poet chooses affects the <u>message</u> of the poem.
>
> 2)  Poets sometimes deliberately <u>break the rules</u> of how a particular form should be written in order to get their <u>message</u> across.

## Ballads *tell a* Story

### The Charge of the Light Brigade (Pages 6-7)

1)  Ballad forms were used to tell <u>stories</u> in a memorable way through strong images. The poet clearly wants the reader to <u>remember</u> the sacrifice made by the Light Brigade.

2)  The <u>endings</u> of ballads often contained a <u>moral message</u>. In this poem the poet makes it clear that we should <u>respect</u> the sacrifice made by the men — he tells us to "Honour the Light Brigade".

3)  Like many ballads, it has a <u>refrain</u>. It emphasises "the six hundred" to remind us of them.

### The Yellow Palm (Pages 24-25)

1)  This poem uses a more <u>modern</u> ballad form in the <u>first person</u>.

2)  Using a <u>refrain</u>, "As I made my way down Palestine Street", reminds the reader that <u>destruction</u> and <u>distress</u> are in all aspects of daily life.

Jessica refrained from telling Liz that crop tops went out of fashion years ago.

## Sonnets *are usually about* Love

### next to of course god america i (Pages 14-15)

1)  Traditionally, sonnets were used to write <u>love poetry</u>. Here the subject is apparently <u>patriotic love</u> for one's country — "america i / love you".

2)  The poem <u>doesn't</u> use the traditional sonnet <u>rhythm</u>. This emphasises the way the speaker seems to be <u>gabbling</u> and jumbling together scraps of patriotic jargon.

3)  There's a <u>regular rhyme scheme</u>, which is normal for a sonnet, but in this case it could be <u>ironic</u> considering the <u>jumbled up</u> ideas that support it.

4)  Usually the final couplet <u>sums up</u> the idea of a sonnet. Here, the final line changes to the third person and makes the reader look more <u>objectively</u> at the speaker — he seems nervous and insincere.

## Tercets *are stanzas with* Three Lines

### Flag (Pages 18-19)

1)  The poet uses each tercet to set up a <u>pattern</u> for the poem.

2)  The tercet pattern makes the poem's ideas <u>clear</u>. The <u>contrast</u> between the trivial cloth and the <u>extreme</u> things people will do for it is emphasised by the <u>short</u> lines and <u>repeated</u> pattern.

3)  The final stanza <u>changes</u> the pattern slightly so that the poem's message has more <u>impact</u>. The speaker warns that wanting a share of the power of the flag will mean a <u>moral compromise</u>.

## 'Futility' *is also written as a sonnet...*

'Futility' uses the traditional 14-line sonnet structure and the meaning is summed up in the final couplet, which is typical of sonnets. It's about sadness and distress rather than love though.

# Poetic Devices

Poets use all kinds of devices to improve their poetry — but not the kind you need a manual for.

> 1) **Enjambment** means <u>carrying on</u> a sentence or phrase over more than one line. It can be used to draw the reader's <u>attention</u> to important ideas.
>
> 2) **Repetition** also makes sure that the reader <u>notices</u> key ideas.

## Enjambment *draws attention to* Words *and* Ideas

### Bayonet Charge (Pages 10-11)

1) The <u>enjambment</u> at the end of most of the lines emphasises the soldier's <u>panic</u> and keeps the pace of the poem <u>fast</u>, as if he can't stop or control himself.

2) The soldier stumbles "towards a green hedge". This doesn't sound threatening until the sentence <u>continues</u> on the next line — it "dazzled with rifle fire". This creates <u>shock</u>.

3) In the middle stanza, his <u>confusion</u> makes him almost <u>stop</u> and wonder why he is there. A <u>caesura</u> pauses the action for this, then the <u>horror</u> starts again with "a yellow hare that rolled like a flame".

### Belfast Confetti (Pages 30-31)

1) The poet mixes <u>enjambment</u> and <u>end stopping</u> to suggest someone coming up against <u>dead ends</u>.

2) When the speaker asks, "What is / My name?" the enjambment creates a <u>pause</u> in what should be a <u>simple</u> question, to show how <u>uncertain</u> he has become.

3) <u>End stopping</u> in lines 13-14 links to the effects of the <u>road blocks</u> making him feel <u>trapped</u>.

### Hawk Roosting (Pages 16-17)

1) Enjambment creates <u>suspense</u> followed by a brutal, <u>shocking</u> extra detail in the lines, "the one path of my flight is direct / Through the bones of the living."

2) The enjambment makes the hawk sound as though he is taking his time and enjoying being in <u>control</u> — "Now I hold Creation in my foot / Or fly up, and revolve it all slowly". The slow pace of long sentences creates a <u>confident</u>, measured feeling.

## Repetition *emphasises* Key Ideas

### The Right Word (Pages 26-27)

1) The speaker repeats the idea of someone "<u>Outside the door</u>" — changing the phrase slightly each time — to emphasise the way that words can create <u>barriers</u> between people.

2) At the end of the poem she repeats the words "<u>Come in</u>". The <u>contrast</u> with "outside" shows that things can <u>change</u> if we change the way we behave.

### 'Come On, Come Back' (Pages 8-9)

1) The <u>title</u> of the poem is <u>repeated</u> several times and turns out to be a song which is "Favourite of all the troops of all the armies". This emphasises the <u>common humanity</u> of enemy troops.

2) The poem <u>ends</u> with the title repeated as its last line. It reminds the reader that Vaudevue, and many others, <u>never</u> did come back. This makes the poem end on a <u>melancholy</u> and <u>wistful</u> note.

## Other poems use interesting sentence structure...

Repetition of words and phrases like "half a league", "cannon" and "the six hundred" in 'The Charge of the Light Brigade' suggest that the events that are described in the poem are inevitable.

# Poetic Devices

Even more poetic devices — hurray...

> 1) Sound effects like <u>alliteration</u> produce a particular <u>effect</u> in a poem.
>
> 2) Other language features like unusual or unexpected <u>vocabulary</u> can also add extra <u>impact</u> to a poem.

## Poetic Devices can Add to the Emotion of a poem

### Mametz Wood (Pages 22-23)

1) <u>Assonance</u> and <u>alliteration</u> create specific <u>sounds</u> throughout the poem. "A chit of bone, the china plate of a shoulder blade", sounds like the <u>plough</u> striking the fragments of the soldiers' skeletons.

2) The <u>alliteration</u> in the poem gives some of the phrases a more <u>determined</u>, energetic feeling. The earth "stands sentinel" and is like "a wound working a foreign body to the surface of the skin".

3) Words with <u>double meanings</u> intensify the thoughtful tone of the poem. The "<u>relic</u> of a finger" associates the soldiers with <u>saintliness</u>, and the "<u>foreign body</u>" is the body of a <u>foreign soldier</u>.

### The Falling Leaves (Pages 12-13)

1) The poet uses <u>alliteration</u> to describe the leaves falling "When no wind whirled them whistling to the sky". This creates a sense of <u>movement</u> which contrasts with what she notices on "a still afternoon" and makes the scene even more <u>silent</u> and strange.

2) <u>Assonance</u> is used to <u>emphasise</u> an important idea in the poem. The soldiers "now all withering lay, / Slain" — the assonance of "lay" and "slain" puts the emphasis on these words, making the description more <u>shocking</u>.

## Unusual Vocabulary can Reinforce the poet's Point

### next to of course god america i (Pages 14-15)

1) The poem mixes <u>rhetorical</u>, <u>persuasive</u> language with casual <u>slang</u>. The speaker seems to be trying to appeal to <u>everyone</u> by using a range of language styles, but it suggests he's <u>insincere</u>.

2) Using <u>incomplete</u> lines from famous songs makes the speaker sound <u>incoherent</u>.

3) Some phrases are <u>distorted</u> — e.g. "deafanddumb" and "by gorry" — as if the speaker is not really thinking about what the things he says actually <u>mean</u>.

4) Some phrases sound very <u>old-fashioned</u> and <u>formal</u> — e.g. "thy sons acclaim your glorious name". The speaker is relying on traditional associations to <u>reassure</u> his audience and sound <u>important</u>.

### 'Come On, Come Back' (Pages 8-9)

1) Using <u>unfamiliar</u> names like "Vaudevue" and "M.L.5" reinforces the <u>strangeness</u> of the setting.

2) <u>Adjectives</u> in <u>unusual contexts</u> make the reader think about what they're describing. The lake is "adorable" despite the danger it holds, and Vaudevue weeps for her "ominous mind".

3) Long sentences and alliteration change the <u>pace</u> of the poem. It speeds up when Vaudevue goes in to the lake — "She strips her uniform off, strips, stands and plunges", creating sudden <u>drama</u>.

## 'Out of the Blue' also uses these language features...

Alliteration in 'Out of the Blue' makes the reader focus on important movements such as "twirling, turning" and "wind-milling, wheeling". Repetition intensifies the narrator's emotions.

# Rhyme and Rhythm

Rhyming is fun — rhyme, time, slime, crime... Nothing really rhymes with "rhythm" though.

> 1) Rhyme and rhythm have an effect on how a poem <u>sounds</u>, which can add to the <u>meaning</u>.
>
> 2) They can also be used to <u>emphasise</u> key words and ideas.

## Some poems have a Regular Rhyme and Rhythm

### The Charge of the Light Brigade (Pages 6-7)

1) The poet uses <u>regular rhythm</u> all the way through the poem to suggest a sense of the <u>energy</u> and <u>speed</u> of the cavalry charging forward into battle.

2) The metre is mainly <u>dactylic</u> — one <u>stressed</u> syllable followed by two <u>unstressed</u> ones. This creates a <u>galloping</u> effect, like the sound of horses' hooves.

3) All the stanzas contain <u>rhymes</u> and <u>half rhymes</u> such as "onward", "blunder'd" and "thunder'd", which emphasise the <u>final rhyme</u> in each stanza and the <u>number</u> of men involved.

4) The repetition of rhymes within and across stanzas reflects the <u>noise</u> of the battle.

### The Yellow Palm (Pages 24-25)

A slow pace can be annoying if you're in a hurry.

1) The second, fourth and sixth lines in each six-line stanza rhyme. This helps to <u>emphasise</u> the <u>final line</u> in each stanza — usually the ones that mention a negative detail.

2) The poet uses rhyme to highlight <u>key words</u> and ideas. He rhymes "prayer" with "despair" and "smile" with "missile" to show how <u>fractured</u> the city has been by war.

3) The rhythm of each stanza is fairly regular and creates a <u>slow pace</u>. This reinforces the idea of the narrator <u>stopping</u> every so often to observe another detail of the city.

## Irregular rhyme and rhythm Add to the Meaning of poems

### 'Come On, Come Back' (Pages 8-9)

1) The rhyme and rhythm in the poem are <u>irregular</u> — this reflects the <u>confused</u> mind of Vaudevue.

2) The occasional rhymes are <u>unexpected</u>. The poet rhymes "feet" and "beat" in a couplet to create a sense of the regular movement of the <u>waves</u>, which contrasts with Vaudevue's <u>vagueness</u>.

3) Half rhymes and internal rhymes create an <u>eerie</u> tone and emphasise the imagery in "At midnight in the moonlight" and "The waters on each side of the moony track / Are black as her mind".

### Out of the Blue (Pages 20-21)

1) A <u>mixture</u> of rhyme and internal rhyme reflects a large scene with <u>small details</u>.

2) He uses rhyme to <u>emphasise</u> some of the harsher words such as "driving" and "diving".

3) <u>Rhymes</u> within a sentence — e.g. "leaving, diving" — give the reader a sense of <u>urgency</u>.

4) The poet uses rhyme and half rhyme to suggest <u>tumbling</u> from a great height — "wind-milling, wheeling, spiralling, falling." The slow rhythm of the <u>long vowel sounds</u> also adds to this.

## 'Futility' uses half rhyme instead of perfect rhyme...

'Futility' mostly uses half rhyme (e.g. "seeds" and "sides"), but the final line of each stanza rhymes with the fifth line. This produces a sense of completeness at the end of each stanza.

# Use of First Person

Lots of poets use a first person, "I" narrator to get their message across more strongly.

> 1) The perspective the poem is narrated from affects the way it comes across to the reader.
> 2) A first person narrator often makes a poem seem more personal and emotional.
> 3) Description using the first person may be more one-sided than third person descriptions.

## First Person Narration *can seem more Personal*

### Poppies (Pages 32-33)

1) The character speaking in this poem is a mother whose son has left home to join the army.
2) The use of the first person allows the poet to express the mother's intense emotions, e.g. "I was brave, as I walked / with you, to the front door". The poem seems very personal and intimate, as if she is expressing her most private thoughts.
3) The poem also gives a voice to other mothers and families left behind by soldiers. Using the first person makes the details sound convincing but there is a sense that she is speaking for mothers everywhere.

### Out of the Blue (Pages 20-21)

1) Using the first person makes the character's horror seem more real and distressing. It reminds the reader that the victims of the World Trade Centre attacks were all individuals with lives and families, not just tiny figures on a television screen.
2) The narrator addresses a loved one directly by asking, "Do you see me, my love".
3) The first person voice gives the reader an insight into the changing emotions of someone trapped in the disaster. The narrator starts off sounding quite determined — "the white of surrender is not yet flying" — but then begins to lose hope and is "tiring, tiring".

### The Right Word (Pages 26-27)

1) The poem is in the first person but the speaker could represent anyone, including the reader. The poet emphasises this by repeating personal pronouns — "I", "my", "mine", "your" and "you".
2) The speaker asks the reader directly, "Is that the wrong description?", which makes the reader consider the idea that words can be misleading and confusing.

## But First Person Narrators *can be Unreliable*

### Hawk Roosting (Pages 16-17)

1) The poem is written in the voice of a hawk. The language it uses is deliberately blunt and measured, to create a sense of the hawk's power.
2) Although the hawk is giving its view of the world, the way the poem is written makes it obvious that it is deluded and over-confident.
3) The hawk sounds arrogant and self-centred. The first and last lines of the poem begin with "I" and the words "me" and "my" are repeated several times throughout the poem.

## Changing a poem's perspective can change its meaning...

If 'At the Border, 1979' had been narrated from the mother's point of view rather than the child's, the effect of the poem would have been to praise her homeland rather than to criticise borders.

# Beginnings of Poems

Poets have to make sure that the beginning of the poem makes us want to keep reading.

> 1) The beginning of the poem is important because it <u>sets the tone</u> for the rest of the poem.
>
> 2) Poets try to get the reader's <u>attention</u> straight away, using techniques like <u>addressing</u> the reader directly or introducing <u>mysterious</u> elements that the reader will want to find out more about.

## Beginnings can be <u>Dramatic</u>

### Futility (Pages 4-5)

1) This poem <u>involves</u> the reader immediately by beginning with an <u>order</u>. This suggests that the speaker is someone who is used to being in command, like an army officer.

2) The <u>beginning</u> of the poem creates questions in the reader's mind — the pronoun "him" is <u>mysterious</u>, and we have to <u>guess</u> who the character is and why he can't move himself.

3) The second line begins with the word "Gently", which <u>contrasts</u> with the command in the first line. It implies tenderness and <u>peace</u> as the narrator describes how the soldier's life used to be.

### Bayonet Charge (Pages 10-11)

1) The poem begins with the word "<u>Suddenly</u>", which establishes the sense of <u>urgency</u> and panic that the soldier is feeling.

2) It starts in the middle of the <u>action</u>, putting the reader in the same <u>confused</u> position as the soldier who "awoke" to find himself in a battle.

Mopsy only liked poems with dramatic beginnings.

## Beginnings can establish a <u>Theme</u>

### Mametz Wood (Pages 22-23)

1) The poem begins with the idea that something else has <u>already happened</u>. The word "afterwards" refers to the <u>war</u>, but that might not be obvious to start with.

2) The poet uses a <u>pronoun</u> — "them" — to make the reader wonder who this refers to. The answer — "the wasted young" — is <u>shocking</u> compared to the relaxed feel of the opening.

3) The farmers are finding the remains of dead soldiers. This introduces an image of <u>quiet horror</u> into the poem.

4) The first stanza introduces the idea of <u>damage</u> and loss. The word "wasted" suggests decay and <u>pointless loss</u> of young lives.

5) The farmers "tended the land back into itself". This introduces the idea that it has been injured and <u>corrupted</u> by the fighting, which is described in more detail later in the poem.

## 'The Charge of the Light Brigade' has a good beginning too...

The opening lines of 'The Charge of the Light Brigade' — "Half a league, half a league, / Half a league onward" — give the impression of rushing non-stop towards their impending doom.

# Couplets and Last Lines

Last lines are pretty <u>important</u> too...

> 1) The last line of a poem's important, because the reader's most likely to <u>remember</u> the ending.
>
> 2) Poets might try to <u>sum up</u> the poem at the end so that the reader remembers the <u>message</u>.

## Closing couplets can Sum Up a Message

### The Charge of the Light Brigade (Pages 6-7)

1) The last line sums up how the Light Brigade should be <u>remembered</u> — as the "<u>Noble</u> six hundred!".

2) The exclamation makes the adjective "Noble" very <u>definite</u> and emphatic.

3) The poet uses a <u>rhyming couplet</u> just before the last line. The rhyme and repetition emphasise the command to "<u>Honour</u> the Light Brigade".

4) The rhyming couplet maintains the <u>rhythm</u> of the poem, making it <u>energetic</u> right up to the last line.

### Flag (Pages 18-19)

1) The final couplet of the poem sounds very <u>sarcastic</u> and <u>cynical</u>.

2) The couplet is used in a traditional way to <u>sum up</u> and emphasise the message of the poem. The speaker is warning the listener that too much <u>loyalty</u> to a country's flag can make people do <u>immoral</u> things — "blind your conscience to the end".

3) Making the last two lines a rhyming couplet is a <u>change</u> from the rhyme scheme of the previous stanzas. It makes the ending sound more <u>definite</u> and uncompromising, to suggest that patriotism and immoral actions are closely <u>linked</u>.

## Endings can Create a Contrast

### At the Border, 1979 (Pages 28-29)

1) The last line in this poem uses an image of a "<u>chain of mountains</u>" to sum up the poet's <u>message</u> about man-made borders. The word "chain" reminds the reader of the "thick iron chain" earlier on in the poem which was <u>restricting</u> the family.

2) However, this chain of mountains "encompassed all of us" — it <u>joins</u> people rather than dividing them.

3) The tone is <u>simple</u> and <u>confident</u>, pointing out how <u>artificial</u> national boundaries and borders are.

4) The <u>straightforward</u>, <u>factual</u> feel of the final statement makes the behaviour of people earlier on in the poem seem <u>over-emotional</u>.

### The Yellow Palm (Pages 24-25)

1) The poem ends with an image of <u>innocence</u> and simplicity. The picture of the child reaching out and receiving fruit is a <u>contrast</u> to the way war has complicated so many other areas of society.

2) The language is <u>plain</u>. The poet could be suggesting that a simple change in <u>behaviour</u> could be a <u>solution</u> to the miseries of war.

3) The last line also reminds the reader that the <u>beauty</u> of nature can be <u>obscured</u> by human conflict.

## Other poems have significant last lines...

The final couplet in 'Out of the Blue' emphasises "sagging" and "flagging", making the narrator sound defeated. 'Futility' ends with a rhetorical question that challenges the reader.

# Imagery

They say a picture paints a thousand words. Well, sometimes words can paint a picture too...

> 1) Imagery is language that describes a particular <u>sense</u>
>    — sight, smell, sound, taste or touch.
> 2) <u>Metaphors</u> and <u>similes compare</u> the thing being described to something else.

## Imagery can be Violent

### Bayonet Charge (Pages 10-11)

1) The imagery in this poem is <u>violent</u> and <u>painful</u>. Similes like "lugged a rifle numb as a smashed arm" suggest <u>pain</u> and blur the distinction between weapons and bodies.

2) The poet uses images that draw on the <u>physical senses</u> — e.g. "dazzled with rifle fire", "Bullets smacking the belly out of the air", "blue crackling air" — and sound both exciting and horrific.

3) The poet uses a metaphor to describe the "cold clockwork of the stars and the nations". This puts the soldier in a <u>wider context</u> — it makes him seem very <u>insignificant</u>.

4) The metaphor of the soldier's "<u>terror's touchy dynamite</u>" in the last line reinforces the <u>panic</u> that the soldier is experiencing, and the idea that this could lead to <u>disaster</u>.

### Belfast Confetti (Pages 30-31)

Nicki mixed weapon imagery with eccentric clothes and make up.

1) The narrator in this poem uses the imagery of <u>writing</u> to explain the experience of being caught up in <u>violence</u> in Belfast. He makes language seem <u>aggressive</u> and dangerous.

2) "A fount of broken type" and "it was raining exclamation marks" describe the painful <u>shrapnel</u> and <u>debris</u> from the explosion which shower down on him. The explosion is "an asterisk on the map" — an asterisk looks like an <u>explosion</u> seen from above.

3) He mixes <u>language</u> and <u>weapon</u> imagery to describe his experiences. The metaphor "A fusillade of question-marks" makes it sound like he is being <u>attacked by language</u>. This suggests that orders and instructions can <u>control</u> and imprison us.

## Images can create a Reflective mood

### Mametz Wood (Pages 22-23)

1) The imagery makes the soldiers' bones sound <u>fragile</u> and <u>delicate</u> — e.g. "the blown / and broken bird's egg of a skull" and "the china plate of a shoulder blade".

2) The poet uses the image of a <u>wound</u> "working a foreign body to the surface of the skin" to describe the soldiers' remains being unearthed — as if the land wants them to be <u>discovered</u>.

3) The poet combines images of <u>horror</u> and <u>beauty</u>. He talks about "the notes they had sung", which sounds gentle, but their "absent tongues" remind the reader that they have rotted away.

4) The <u>oxymoron</u> "nesting machine guns" combines a <u>natural</u> image of protection with the <u>violence</u> of war to show how the natural landscape has been <u>corrupted</u>.

5) The poet uses some striking and <u>disturbing</u> visual imagery like the soldiers who "paused mid <u>dance-macabre</u>", as if in a medieval dance of death.

## 'Poppies' and 'The Falling Leaves' also use imagery...

Military imagery in 'Poppies' reminds us that the son is going to war, and the mother uses domestic imagery to describe her fear. In 'The Falling Leaves', leaves and snowflakes represent dead soldiers.

# Irony

Like rain on your wedding day... (That's actually not ironic at all, just bad luck.)

> 1) Poems are ironic if what a narrator or character says is <u>different</u> from what they <u>mean</u>.
>
> 2) Poets often use irony to make <u>views</u> that they strongly <u>disagree</u> with seem <u>ridiculous</u>.

## These poems treat Patriotism in an Ironic way

### Flag (Pages 18-19)

1) The poem suggests it's ironic that even though a flag is "just a piece of <u>cloth</u>" it can have such <u>power</u> over human behaviour that it can bring "a nation to its knees".

2) The speaker uses an <u>ironic</u> and <u>patronising tone</u> when he says that to possess something so powerful, all his questioner has to do is "just ask for a flag, my friend".

3) The speaker suggests that people need to <u>ignore</u> what's right to use the power, and tells the listener to "<u>blind your conscience</u> to the end". This is ironic advice that shows his <u>contempt</u> for the flag.

### next to of course god america i (Pages 14-15)

1) The poem is written in an ironic way. The speaker in the poem is trying to seem <u>inspirational</u> and earnest, but the poet wants the reader to see him as <u>insincere</u>.

2) The speaker says "we should worry" after he's spoken of the centuries that have passed. He is being <u>sarcastic</u>, but the poet is suggesting that leaders have a <u>careless</u> attitude towards history.

3) At the end of his speech the speaker asks "then shall the voice of liberty be mute?". It's meant to be a stirring <u>rhetorical question</u> that inspires his audience to support him, but it's ironic because the line before is all about how those who have fought before are <u>dead</u> — their voices are <u>mute</u>.

### At the Border, 1979 (Pages 28-29)

1) The irony is that the <u>adults</u> in the poem are very <u>emotional</u> about crossing the border back to their homeland, while the narrator can see that the land in both countries is <u>the same</u>.

2) The narrator reports what her parents have told her in a <u>straightforward</u> way that makes them seem a bit <u>silly</u>. E.g. It seems unlikely that "soon everything would taste different".

3) The poet uses <u>hyperbole</u> for the words of the mother. She says that in their homeland "the roads are <u>much cleaner</u>", the landscape "<u>more beautiful</u>" and the people "<u>much kinder</u>".

4) The last line sums up the irony — "The <u>same</u> chain of mountains encompassed all of us."

## Irony can Emphasise Violence and Horror

### Belfast Confetti (Pages 30-31)

1) The <u>title</u> of this poem is ironic. Confetti is associated with <u>celebration</u> and happiness, especially at weddings, which usually <u>unite</u> people. But "Belfast Confetti" refers to <u>shrapnel</u> of bombs and the <u>division</u> that results.

2) It's ironic that the character in the poem can list the names of <u>military equipment</u> e.g."Saracen" and "Kremlin-2 mesh" but he can't remember his own <u>name</u> or where he is going.

## 'Come On, Come Back' is ironic too...

'Come On, Come Back' shows that it's ironic that people join enemy armies when they have some things in common — Vaudevue and the enemy sentinel have the same favourite song.

# Mood

After all this revision I'd guess you're in a pretty bad mood...

> 1) Mood in poetry is about the <u>tone</u> or <u>atmosphere</u> of the poem.
>
> 2) Most of the poems to do with conflict have a <u>sad</u> or <u>angry</u> tone because they deal with a <u>negative topic</u>.

## Most *of these poems have a* Sad Mood

### Futility (Pages 4-5)

1) The mood of this poem is one of <u>sadness</u> at the waste of human life in war.

2) The narrator's tone becomes more <u>bitter</u> and <u>disillusioned</u> as the poem goes on. He begins by referring to the "kind old sun" but by the end he is <u>criticising</u> the "fatuous sunbeams".

3) The poem develops a <u>challenging</u> tone as the speaker asks what is the point of life when it can be so easily destroyed by war. The final rhetorical question sounds <u>angry</u>.

### 'Come On, Come Back' (Pages 8-9)

1) The mood of the poem is <u>sad</u> and <u>wistful</u> for Vaudevue's lost life.

2) By the end of the poem, the title "Come On, Come Back" seems to be a <u>melancholy</u> call to all the troops whose lives have been <u>destroyed</u>.

3) There is a strong atmosphere of <u>loneliness</u> and <u>isolation</u>. Vaudevue's mind is "secret from her". The enemy sentinel waits <u>alone</u> for her return, which never happens. Her clothes are "<u>abandoned</u>".

4) The waters that Vaudevue drowns in are <u>welcoming</u> to her but the description of them also creates a <u>sinister</u> mood. They are "black as her mind", and the undercurrent is "treacherous" and "icy".

Meg preferred a mood of loud sadness.

### The Falling Leaves (Pages 12-13)

1) This poem has a mood of <u>quiet sadness</u>.

2) The focus is on <u>death</u> right from the beginning. The poet describes the dead "brown leaves dropping" like the soldiers who "all withering lay".

3) The images of the leaves falling <u>in silence</u> and the snowflakes "wiping out the noon" creates an <u>eerie</u> atmosphere in the middle of the poem.

4) There is a tone of <u>respect</u> and <u>admiration</u> for the men. The poet calls them a "gallant multitude" and refers to their "beauty" which has been <u>lost too soon</u>.

## Some *have an* Anxious Mood

### Poppies (Pages 32-33)

1) The poem starts in a <u>solemn</u> mood. It is "Three days before Armistice Sunday", which immediately reminds the reader of all the people who have <u>died</u> in wars.

2) The mother in the poem wants to express her real feelings but she <u>hides</u> her emotions from her son.

3) There is an atmosphere of <u>restrained fear</u> and <u>anxiety</u> in the poem.

4) The mother's mood <u>contrasts</u> with the son's <u>excitement</u> and exhilaration — he is "intoxicated".

## All poems have a mood...

The mood of 'Flag' is calm and sarcastic; the mood of 'The Charge of the Light Brigade' is respectful and admiring; the mood of 'Bayonet Charge' and 'Belfast Confetti' is fearful and panicky.

# The Poetry Exam: Unit Two Overview

If you're following <u>Route A</u> of the AQA English Literature course, you'll have to do an <u>exam</u> called <u>Unit 2: Poetry Across Time</u>.  That's what this page is all about.

## Your Exam <u>*Will be* Split Up</u> <u>*Like This*</u>

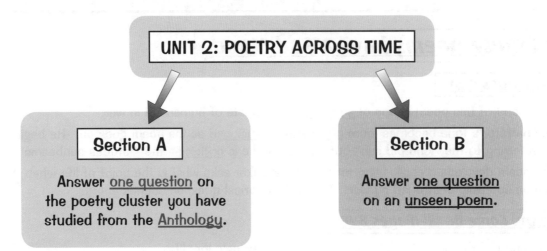

UNIT 2: POETRY ACROSS TIME

### Section A
Answer <u>one question</u> on the poetry cluster you have studied from the <u>Anthology</u>.

### Section B
Answer <u>one question</u> on an <u>unseen poem</u>.

1)  This guide contains all the poems from the '<u>Conflict</u>' cluster of the Anthology — this should be the one you've studied in class.  There are three other poetry clusters, which you <u>don't</u> need to <u>worry about</u>.

2)  The next few pages will give you <u>tips</u> on how to answer the question in <u>Section A</u>.

3)  Section A is worth <u>two-thirds</u> of the marks in the <u>exam</u> and nearly a <u>quarter</u> of your entire <u>GCSE</u>.

## This is How Your Exam <u>*Will Work*</u>

1)  The whole exam lasts <u>1 hour 15 minutes</u>.  You should spend about <u>45 minutes</u> on <u>Section A</u>.  The other 30 minutes should be spent doing Section B.

2)  Section A has a <u>choice</u> of <u>two questions</u> for each poetry cluster.  You should only answer <u>one question</u> and it should be about the cluster you've <u>studied</u>.  The question is worth <u>36 marks</u>.

3)  You're <u>not allowed</u> to take your <u>own anthology</u> or any <u>notes</u> about the poems into the exam.  You'll be given a <u>blank copy</u> of the anthology to help you with your answer.

4)  You'll also be given a <u>separate answer book</u> to write your answer in.

## There are <u>Instructions</u> <u>*on the* Front Page</u> <u>*of the* Exam</u>

1)  You <u>must read</u> the <u>front page</u> of the exam paper <u>before</u> you start — it tells you <u>exactly</u> what to do.

2)  There will be a <u>list</u> of things you need for the exam.  Make sure you've got <u>everything</u> on it.

3)  Check you've got the <u>right exam paper</u> — it should be the one for the <u>higher tier</u>.

4)  Remember to fill in <u>all the details</u> on the front page of the <u>answer booklet</u>.

## I hope you're paying attention — there's an exam on this...
I like pages like this.  Absolutely <u>no learning</u> whatsoever.  Lovely.  Don't worry if you forget some of this stuff — there'll be a <u>reminder</u> of how the exam works on the <u>front page</u> of the exam paper.

# Sample Question 1

OK, so now you know what the exam's about. I bet you're just dying to find out what the questions will be like, eh? Er, well... Here's your first sample question anyway.

## Read the Question Carefully and Underline Key Words

1) You'll have a choice of two questions, so it's best to read them both through carefully first. Then pick the one you think you've got the best chance of answering well.

2) Once you've done that, read the question you've chosen through again. Underline the question's theme and any other important words.

3) The question will give you the title of one poem and ask you to compare it to one other poem of your choice. Pick another poem you think relates to the theme.

4) Look up the poems you're going to write about in the blank copy of the anthology you'll be given in the exam. Turn over the corners of the pages they're on so you can find them again quickly.

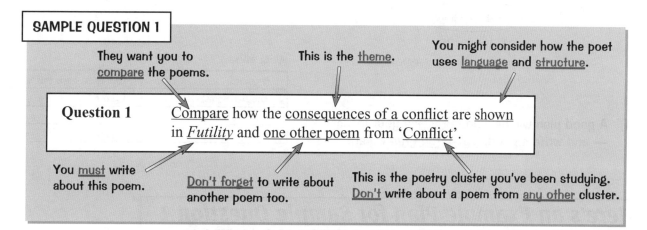

SAMPLE QUESTION 1

They want you to compare the poems.

This is the theme.

You might consider how the poet uses language and structure.

**Question 1**    Compare how the consequences of a conflict are shown in *Futility* and one other poem from 'Conflict'.

You must write about this poem.

Don't forget to write about another poem too.

This is the poetry cluster you've been studying. Don't write about a poem from any other cluster.

## There are Three Main Ways to Get Marks

Whichever question you choose to answer, you'll get marks for:

① Giving your own thoughts and opinions on the poems and supporting them with quotes from the text.

② Explaining features like form, structure and language.

③ Describing the similarities and differences between poems.

In 18th century Scotland, the penalty for forgetting to include quotes was severe.

Keep these three things in mind when you're writing and planning your answer.

## Read the question carefully...

If only I'd always followed that particular piece of advice myself — there might never have been that unfortunate incident with the policeman and the chocolate orange. Still, we live and learn.

# Planning

If you were to ask me what my <u>best tip</u> would be for getting <u>great marks</u> in your exam, I would <u>not</u> say "bribe the examiner". Oh no. That would be <u>wrong</u>. I'd say "<u>plan your essay answer</u>".

## Spend *Five Minutes Planning* Your Answer

1) Always <u>plan</u> your answer <u>before</u> you start — that way, you're less likely to forget something <u>important</u>.

2) Write your plan at the <u>top of your answer booklet</u> and draw a <u>neat line</u> through it when you've finished.

3) <u>Don't</u> spend <u>too long</u> on your plan. It's only <u>rough work</u>, so you don't need to write in full sentences. Here are a few <u>examples</u> of different ways you can plan your answer:

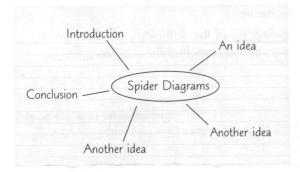

Introduction

An idea

Conclusion — Spider Diagrams

Another idea

Another idea

Bullet points with...
- Intro...
- An idea...
- The next idea...

Tables with...

| A point... | Quote to back this up... |
|---|---|
| Another point... | Quote... |
| A different point... | Quote... |
| A brand new point... | Quote... |

4) A good plan will help you <u>organise</u> your ideas — and write a good, <u>well-structured</u> essay.

## Here's an *Example Plan* for *Sample Question 1*

Here's a <u>possible plan</u> for <u>Sample Question 1</u>. When you're writing your plan, remember to keep in mind the <u>three main ways</u> to get <u>marks</u> from p.55. And keep it <u>brief</u>.

<u>Plan:</u> poem 1 = Futility, poem 2 = Mametz Wood

<u>1) Introduction</u> — kind of consequences in each poem
- Poem 1 — World War I poet's comrade mortally wounded
- Poem 2 — unearthed long-forgotten remains, also from World War I

<u>2) Language Comparison</u>
- Poem 1 — imagery showing care and compassion — 'kind'
- Poem 2 — imagery showing loss, futility, emptiness, fragility — 'wasted', 'broken bird's egg'

<u>3) Form and Structure Comparison</u>
- Poem 1 — partial rhymes, similar to a sonnet, specific to general observations
- Poem 2 — no regular rhyme scheme, short 3-line stanzas, clear statements

<u>4) Wider Issues</u> — why poem was written
- Poem 1 — explores futility of war through death of comrade
- Poem 2 — reconnects with past through rediscovery of lost war graves

<u>5) Summary</u> — Comparing — 'Both these poems...'

Use your plan to start making links between the poems.

Jot down any good quotes you want to use.

Don't forget to write about language, structure and form.

Write about ideas and attitudes too.

## You can't write a great essay without a good plan...

This is time well spent — <u>five minutes</u> spent <u>planning your answer</u> in an exam will help you get a much <u>better mark</u>. <u>Practise</u> by planning your own answers to the sample questions in this guide.

# Mark Scheme

If I were you, I'd be <u>pretty keen</u> to find out what the <u>examiner</u> expected of me right about now. Oh yes, it'd definitely feature somewhere in my <u>top 20</u> things to do when bored. Maybe top 50.

## Look at What You Have to Do to Get Each Grade

Seriously, it's dead <u>important</u> to know <u>what you have to do</u> to get the <u>grade</u> you're aiming for.

| Grade | What you've written |
|---|---|
| **A\*** | • Explores several interpretations or meanings in detail<br>• Provides carefully chosen and well-integrated quotes to back up ideas<br>• Compares the poems thoughtfully and in detail, using plenty of evidence<br>• Looks closely at <u>how</u> language, form and structure affect the reader with well-chosen examples<br>• Gives detailed and imaginative ideas about themes, attitudes and feelings<br>• Considers the evidence to come up with conclusions about the poem |
| **A** | • Gives several interpretations or meanings<br>• Provides well-chosen quotes to support ideas<br>• Compares the poems in detail and provides plenty of evidence<br>• Describes <u>how</u> language, form and structure affect the reader, using examples<br>• Looks at themes, attitudes and feelings in detail, again using plenty of evidence |
| **B** | • Thoughtful interpretation of the poems<br>• Supports interpretations with quotes from the text<br>• Provides some well-chosen evidence to support comparisons between the poems<br>• Gives several examples of <u>how</u> language, form and structure affect the reader<br>• Provides some evidence to support ideas about themes, attitudes and feelings |
| **C** | • Comments on several aspects of the poem, e.g. mood, language, feelings, and uses quotes to back the comments up<br>• Makes several comparisons between the poems<br>• Explains <u>how</u> language, form and structure affect the reader<br>• Makes valid comments about themes, attitudes or feelings in the poems |

> You'll also be marked on your <u>spelling</u>, <u>punctuation</u> and <u>grammar</u> and on how you <u>present</u> your work. To get the <u>best marks</u>, your essay should be <u>clearly organised</u> into <u>well-structured</u> paragraphs. It should also be <u>easy</u> to follow and <u>understand</u>.

# How to Answer the Question

Here's an 'A' grade sample answer to the exam question on p.55.

Compare how the consequences of a conflict are shown in
'Futility' and one other poem from 'Conflict'.

**Introduction**

**1**

Consequences are the outcomes and the effects on people of words and actions. In 'Futility', Wilfred Owen reflects on the consequences of war for a soldier who has been killed in a World War I battle, and, by extension for all the soldiers killed in wars. In 'Mametz Wood', Owen Sheers describes the rediscovery of lost World War I war graves in order to remind us of what happened. Both Wilfred Owen and Owen Sheers reflect upon the fragility and preciousness of life and the waste of life that is an inevitable consequence of war.

← It can be a good idea to briefly define key terms in the question.

Both poets use vivid imagery to describe their thoughts and feelings concerning the consequences of war. Wilfred Owen personifies the sun and hopes that the sun can revive — literally bring back to life — his wounded comrade because "its touch awoke him once". The desire to bring life back to his failing body is evident, as is the link between the sun and life itself: "If anything might rouse him now / The kind old sun will know". Wilfred Owen also uses a Biblical metaphor, "Was it for this the clay grew tall?" of God breathing life into clay in order to create man. The poet questions why the life-giving sun created life in the first place, just so that it should be so brutally and prematurely extinguished in battle: "O what made fatuous sunbeams toil / To break earth's sleep at all?" The contrast between "toil", suggesting hard work, and "fatuous", which sounds stupid and careless, leaves a stark impression of the madness of war.

← Talk about similarities and differences between the two poems.

← Back up your points with quotes from the poem.

**Language**

**2**

The language in 'Mametz Wood' also contrasts wholesome images with the horrors of war — there is a clear juxtaposition of farming work and the unearthing of the dead victims of war. The "plough blades", used in turning over the earth ready for planting, unearth "A chit of bone, the china plate of a shoulder blade." The fragility of the remains of the dead — and of life itself — is further emphasised by the continuing description of the exhumed remains: "the blown / and broken bird's egg of a skull". The terrible and pathetic consequences of a brutal conflict are exposed for all to see by this shocking imagery. The bird imagery is continued where the "wasted young" soldiers are ordered towards "nesting machine guns." Nesting is associated with eggs and new life, but here there is only death. 'Mametz Wood' contains vivid, pitiful and sometimes macabre images ending with a description of the jaws of the dead soldiers having dropped open to reveal "their absent tongues." Unlike in 'Futility', flesh and life have long since departed, and now only silence is left, leaving these sad mute witnesses to the lives cut short in 'Mametz Wood'.

← Describe the effect of different images.

← Use effective and varied vocabulary.

# How to Answer the Question

**3 Form and Structure**

The form and structure of both poems also affects the way the consequences of war are presented. 'Futility' is presented almost like a sonnet, but it has two halves and it lacks the traditional sonnet's more rigid formal features. The rhythm is irregular, and the rhymes are mainly half rhymes rather than full rhymes. These irregular rhythms and the "failed" pararhymes, e.g. "once" and "France", reflect the failing life of the dying soldier. The first stanza deals with the specific situation of the dying man and there is still a small amount of hope for a positive outcome. But in the second stanza, the narrator realises that his comrade is beyond human help. This structure enables the poet to conclude with his angry rhetorical question about the consequences of war. 'Mametz Wood', on the other hand, is written in tercets with no regular rhyme scheme. It switches between describing what is happening in the present — the skeletons being discovered — and what happened in the past, with the earth presenting "reminders of what happened", emphasising how the effects of war are long-lasting.

> Write about form.

> Don't just describe the technique — explain its effect too.

**4 Wider Issues**

Although 'Futility' and 'Mametz Wood' focus on different aspects of the consequences of war, they may be seen as complementary works. Wilfred Owen's poem is written with the immediacy of one who, as an officer, experienced directly "this morning" the trench warfare of the Western Front and suffered its horrors and challenges alongside his men. Indeed, tragically, Wilfred Owen himself was killed in action shortly before the war ended. Owen Sheers on the other hand was not a direct witness to the conflict, but the unearthed "wasted young" he describes are themselves proof of past carnage. 'Mametz Wood' was written with the distance and clarity of hindsight; the descriptions of the unearthed dead in this poem are portrayed almost in archaeological terms. Nevertheless, although the distance of time may lend some objectivity to our view, we still find ourselves reacting with feeling to the human tragedy, the lasting consequence of the conflict of war. The image of the earth revealing the dead by "reaching back into itself" suggests that the earth is encouraging us to remember the soldiers who lost their lives in battle.

> Explain and justify your statements and ideas.

> Give your own interpretation of the poem's message.

**5 Conclusion**

It has clearly been shown through these two poems that suffering and tragedy are both consequences of conflict. Each poem is a reflection and meditation on a specific instance of conflict, with graphic descriptions of death shown alongside more philosophical reactions. They elicit our sympathy and oblige us, the readers, to recollect the "Futility" and "the wasted young" of the First World War.

> It's a good idea to end by referring to both poems.

THIS IS A FLAP.
FOLD THIS PAGE OUT.

# Sample Question 2

Okey doke, here's another <u>Sample Question</u> for you — it's <u>number two</u> of <u>three</u>, you lucky thing. Have a think about how <u>you'd</u> answer it, then turn over for an <u>example</u> of how you could do it.

## Here's Sample Question 2

This is another <u>example</u> of the type of question that might come up in your <u>exam</u>. Remember to <u>read</u> the question <u>carefully</u> and <u>underline key words</u>.

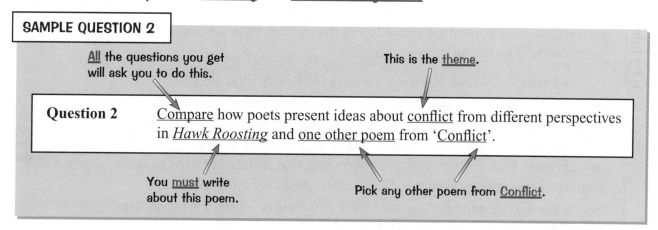

SAMPLE QUESTION 2

<u>All</u> the questions you get will ask you to do this.

This is the <u>theme</u>.

**Question 2**     <u>Compare</u> how poets present ideas about <u>conflict</u> from different perspectives in <u>Hawk Roosting</u> and <u>one other poem</u> from 'Conflict'.

You <u>must</u> write about this poem.

Pick any other poem from <u>Conflict</u>.

## Here's an Example Plan for Sample Question 2

Here's an example of a <u>different way</u> you could plan your answer. Remember, you need to start thinking up <u>comparisons</u> between the poems at the <u>planning stage</u>.

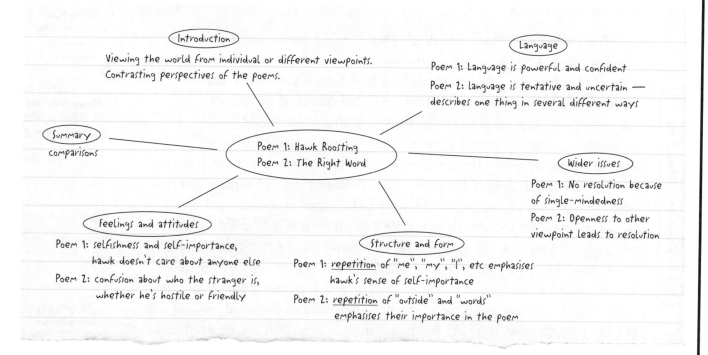

Introduction
Viewing the world from individual or different viewpoints.
Contrasting perspectives of the poems.

Language
Poem 1: Language is powerful and confident
Poem 2: language is tentative and uncertain — describes one thing in several different ways

Summary
comparisons

Poem 1: Hawk Roosting
Poem 2: The Right Word

Wider issues
Poem 1: No resolution because of single-mindedness
Poem 2: Openness to other viewpoint leads to resolution

feelings and attitudes
Poem 1: selfishness and self-importance, hawk doesn't care about anyone else
Poem 2: confusion about who the stranger is, whether he's hostile or friendly

Structure and form
Poem 1: repetition of "me", "my", "I", etc emphasises hawk's sense of self-importance
Poem 2: repetition of "outside" and "words" emphasises their importance in the poem

## Try out different types of plans to see what's best for you...

When you're writing answers to <u>practice exam questions</u>, try doing your <u>plan</u> a bit <u>differently</u> each time — that way, you can work out the <u>best way</u> to <u>organise your ideas</u> before the real thing.

# How to Answer the Question

Here's an 'A' grade sample answer to the exam question on p.59.

Compare how poets present ideas about conflict from different perspectives in 'Hawk Roosting' and one other poem from 'Conflict'.

**1 Introduction**

It is a common observation that people often see the world from a particular point of view and resist opportunities to appreciate different perspectives. Other people are able to see things from other angles. Many poems skilfully and accurately express this.

*Show that you understand the question.*

**2 Language**

Ted Hughes's 'Hawk Roosting' portrays the hawk's utter single-mindedness from the hawk's point of view. It believes that the whole of creation exists for itself alone, and it uses its imagined power to cause conflict and violence — it delights in "perfect kills" and "tearing off heads". The hawk believes that it controls all of creation and that it does not need to use arguments to justify its position. The creature allows no compromise, and has no place in its mind for any alternative perspective: "There is no sophistry in my body." In contrast, 'The Right Word' by Imtiaz Dharker is full of uncertainty and deals with conflict in general rather than the violent attacks described in 'Hawk Roosting'. The language used is tentative as the narrator attempts to define who or what stands outside the door, and questions and different perspectives follow one after the other. The narrator is searching for the "right word", the "right" description for the newcomer. The narrator feels vulnerable and the fear and possibility that the young person will attack seem very real to start with.

*Use quotes to support your ideas.*

**3 Form and Structure**

The structure of 'Hawk Roosting' reflects the single-minded, aloof confidence of the hawk. There are regular stanzas of four lines, almost like a hymn of self-praise. The words referring to the hawk's own self, "me", "mine", "my", "I" occur twenty-one times over the course of the twenty-four line poem. This repetition emphasises the idea that the creature is self-obsessed to an absurd degree. This is clearly where its illusion of power and control stems from. The structure of 'The Right Word', however, helps to reflect the uncertainty of the poet. Each stanza consists of three to five short, abrupt lines expressing on the one hand a sense of menace and dread caused by the stranger "outside that door", and then this is followed by the possibility of sympathy. In each stanza, the narrator alters her opinions and perspective about the young person. She takes up and discards meanings and interpretations of the person one after another in a frustrating search for 'The Right Word'. The perceived threat is clearly expressed in the word "lurking". But the narrator then seems to feel that "terrorist" is an inadequate definition. She later suggests that the young person is a "freedom-fighter", and that, instead of "lurking" the figure is taking shelter in the shadows. In the fourth stanza, the rhetorical question is posed: "Are words no more / than waving,

*Show how structure helps to convey meaning.*

*Always mention the effect of what you're describing.*

*Explain any contradictions.*

*Rhetorical questions drive a point home.*

# How to Answer the Question

wavering flags?" The position of this metaphor, coming after all the failed definitions, suggests that words are merely symbolic and fail to resolve problems.

The emotions in the two poems also show contrasting perspectives towards conflict. The frustration and confusion of the narrator of 'The Right Word' is shown in her constant questions and outbursts like "God help me" — a cry of exasperation at the confusion of words and labels that the narrator is faced with. The uncertain attitude of the narrator in 'The Right Word' is in direct contrast to Ted Hughes's hawk. The hawk has a clear and absolutely constant sense of itself and its purpose. In fact, the hawk is utterly incapable of introspective doubt. It believes the world, the whole of creation exists for its convenience, to facilitate its life. The hawk's self-confidence is absolute and it claims ownership of the whole of nature: "Now I hold Creation in my foot." And its freedom seems absolute: "I kill where I please because it is all mine." In spite of this, the reader is left in no doubt about the foolish and misplaced nature of the hawk's conviction when it states, without a trace of irony "I am going to keep things like this." We know that in the real world this is quite unrealistic and probably impossible.

*Remember to keep making comparisons.*

In 'The Right Word', the narrator's eventual resolution is quite different from that of 'Hawk Roosting'. In 'The Right Word', the narrator's wavering interpretation of the stranger is settled and resolved with compassion and an act of trust. Labels are abandoned and the child outside the door is invited into the home to join in a meal; "a boy who looks like your son, too" steps inside, and with grace and courtesy "carefully, at my door, / takes off his shoes." This is a very humane resolution to the narrator's problem, which implies a resolution to the narrator's issues. The mysterious stranger is no longer threatening after a simple act of friendship and compassion — the welcome of the opened door. Ted Hughes's hawk, because of its arrogance, is not open to this opportunity. Its freedom and its superb adaptation to the conditions that provide "convenience" have blinded it to any criticism.

*Use quotes to support your argument.*

*Expand on the effects of what you've just quoted.*

The protagonist in 'The Right Word' is finally able to escape her fear-driven point of view. In contrast to this we know by the end of the poem that the hawk is a prisoner of its very nature. Its total lack of introspection and inability to see other perspectives have created an illusion which it cannot see beyond. The difference in viewpoint between the two poems shows that conflict can be avoided by considering the feelings and attitudes of other people, as the narrator in 'The Right Word' does. In contrast, 'Hawk Roosting' shows that feelings of superiority and self-importance are likely to lead to conflict.

*Make sure you've answered the question.*

**Feelings and Attitudes** 4 — **Wider Issues** 5 — **Conclusion** 6

# Sample Question 3

Most of the questions you get in the exam will be pretty <u>similar</u>. One or two might <u>look</u> a bit different, but they <u>shouldn't</u> cause you any <u>major problems</u> — just follow the <u>advice</u> on this page.

## Here's <u>Sample Question 3</u>

Some questions are <u>worded</u> a bit <u>differently</u> — don't let them catch you out. Here's an <u>example</u>:

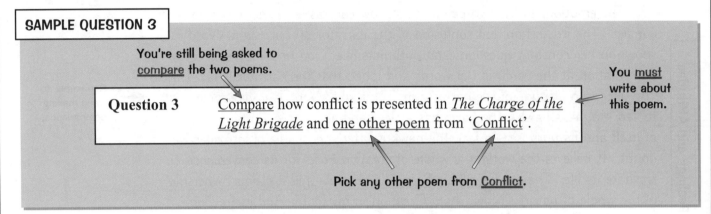

SAMPLE QUESTION 3

You're still being asked to <u>compare</u> the two poems.

You <u>must</u> write about this poem.

**Question 3** <u>Compare</u> how conflict is presented in *The Charge of the Light Brigade* and <u>one other poem</u> from 'Conflict'.

Pick any other poem from <u>Conflict</u>.

## Here's an <u>Example Plan</u> <u>for</u> <u>Sample Question 3</u>

Here's <u>another way</u> you could plan your answer. The table helps you sort out <u>which quotes</u> you want to use to <u>support each of the points</u> you make.

Intro
Poem 1: The Charge of the Light Brigade, Poem 2: Out of the Blue
Response: both poems deal with reactions to conflict

|  | Poem 1 | Poem 2 |
|---|---|---|
| Attitudes towards death | "Theirs not to reason why" | "the white of surrender is not yet flying" |
| Language — repetition | "Half a league, half a league, Half a league onward" | "I am waving, waving" |
| Attitudes towards the characters | "Noble six hundred" | "Does anyone see a soul worth saving?" |

Attitudes toward conflict
The Charge of the Light Brigade — praises soldiers
Out of the Blue — sympathy for victim

## Always write about language, form and structure...

<u>Don't panic</u> — the question looks tricky at first but it's just like the other questions you've seen. Remember to keep comparing the language, form and structure of both poems and you'll be fine.

# The Controlled Assessment

If you're following <u>Route B</u> of the AQA English Literature course, you'll have to do a <u>controlled assessment</u> task for <u>Unit 5: Exploring Poetry</u>. That's what this page is about.

## This is How Unit 5 Works

1) Your teacher will set you a question on some <u>poetry</u>. They might decide to use poems from the poetry <u>Anthology</u> that's covered in this book.

2) The question will ask you to compare <u>contemporary poems</u> (like those in Section 2) with ones from the <u>Literary Heritage</u> (Section 1).

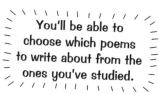
You'll be able to choose which poems to write about from the ones you've studied.

3) You might have to <u>listen to</u> or <u>watch</u> performances of the poems and write about them in your answer.

4) You're expected to write around <u>2000 words</u>. Your answer is worth <u>25%</u> of your <u>final GCSE grade</u>.

## You're Allowed to Plan Your Answer First

1) You'll be able to spend time in class <u>planning</u> and <u>preparing</u> for this essay.

2) During this time, you'll be allowed to look at <u>books</u> and the <u>Internet</u> and <u>ask</u> your teacher <u>questions</u>. You must make a <u>note</u> of anything you use to help you (e.g. a website) in a bibliography.

3) You can write a <u>rough draft</u> if you want, but you <u>won't</u> be able to have it with you while you're writing up your answer. You can take in <u>brief notes</u> though.

## You'll Have up to Four Hours to Write Up Your Answer

1) You can write up your answer in your classroom over a few lessons, but you'll be under <u>exam conditions</u>.

2) You'll be given unmarked <u>copies</u> of the poems to help you.

3) You can write up your essay <u>by hand</u>, or type it up on a <u>computer</u>.

You'll be allowed a <u>dictionary</u> or to use your <u>spell-check</u>, but if you do have a computer you <u>won't</u> be able to get on the <u>Internet</u>.

For Sam's control assessment he had to demonstrate skilful changing of channels.

4) Your work will be <u>collected in</u> at the end of every session. When you've finished, your teacher will collect in <u>everything</u> you've written — including any drafts you did earlier on.

## You'll write up the task under exam conditions...

So, your teacher will set you a <u>question</u> on some poems you've studied. You'll have <u>time</u> to <u>prepare</u> your answer, but you're expected to <u>write it up</u> in a maximum of <u>four</u> supervised hours.

# How to Answer the Question

Here's an 'A' grade sample answer to the exam question on p.62.

<u>Compare how conflict is presented in 'The Charge of the Light Brigade' and one other poem from 'Conflict'.</u>

**Introduction**

**1**

Conflict often has harmful effects, including causing death and destruction, so it is usually viewed negatively. However, conflict can also bring out positive traits in people, and the people involved in it may be respected. 'The Charge of the Light Brigade' and 'Out of the Blue' deal with different types of conflict, and leave the reader with very different impressions of the people involved in it. 'The Charge of the Light Brigade' describes an incident during the Battle of Balaklava and reflects on blind unquestioning obedience and military discipline. 'Out of the Blue' looks at conflict from the perspective of a victim of the September 11th terrorist attacks — it describes the growing panic of impending death and the passive powerlessness of the onlookers.

*Show that you've understood the question.*

*Relate the poem to the incident it's describing.*

**Language**

**2**

The language used in 'Out of the Blue' reflects the terrible predicament of the narrator but also his initial determination. Despite the chaos, he insists that "the white of surrender is not yet flying." We know that he is clinging in vain to hope. He sees the depth beneath him as "appalling" — the repetition of this word emphasises the protagonist's impossible situation. In 'The Charge of the Light Brigade' there is also a sense of determination, but here it is a whole regiment rather than an individual, the "six hundred" and their commanding officer allow no doubts to obscure their duty — "Theirs not to reason why". They see that the situation they face is very dangerous but their duty is clear; so, "Into the valley of Death / Rode the six hundred." This gives the impression that the soldiers were brave enough to face an extremely dangerous situation, but also hints at criticism for the officers who gave the order that would lead to the loss of so many lives. The image of the cavalry riding "Into the mouth of Hell" suggests a predator waiting patiently to consume his prey — it adds to the threatening atmosphere of the poem and warns the reader that the outcome will be tragic.

*Use plenty of embedded quotes.*

*Get extra marks by showing that you understand images and metaphors.*

The form and structure of the poems also plays a part in getting the message across to the reader. 'The Charge of the Light Brigade' has a clear and powerful rhythm and rhyme scheme that suggest the energy of the battle. The Light Brigade's determined gallop towards its destruction is emphasised, by repetition, from the first two lines of the first stanza of the poem: "Half a league, half a league, /

# How to Answer the Question

Form and Structure ③

Half a league onward..." Once the order was given, the fate of the men was sealed — they had no choice but to follow their terrible destiny to its conclusion. The weapons they faced are also repeated, sometimes with slight variations, e.g. "Cannon to right of them, / Cannon to left of them," to emphasise the danger faced by the cavalry and their great bravery. Armitage also uses repetition to suggest inevitability, but in a more spontaneous way. In 'Out of the Blue', desperate actions like "waving, waving" and "tiring, tiring" are repeated, adding to the sense of hopelessness for the character's situation. The tone of the poem becomes more urgent and despairing towards the end as the narrator loses all hope of survival.

> Write about how features like form and structure create an effect.

Feelings and Attitudes ④

The protagonist of 'Out of the Blue' worries that we may misinterpret what we see — he insists, "I am waving, waving" and asks, "Does anyone see / a soul worth saving?" Here there is a sad hint that the victim feels that we may think he is unworthy of being rescued. He is in a life or death predicament, and his actions are about the hopeless hope for life. We are all witnesses to this unfolding drama and the voice of the poem addresses us directly. He pleads, "So when will you come?" but we are helpless. We stand and watch, but can do nothing. This suggests how mass media often makes us feel like helpless witnesses to unspeakable horrors and tragedies. It is clear that Tennyson, on the other hand, wrote 'The Charge of the Light Brigade' as a rousing description of a fruitless but brave sacrifice: "Honour the Light Brigade, / Noble six hundred!" The final exclamation mark further emphasises the poem's message. The initial order given to the Light Brigade was open to doubt and misinterpretation, but we are shown that doubt did not get in the way of honour and the soldiers' sense of duty.

> Show that you're aware of the emotive power of language.

> Get more marks by giving a personal response.

> Show that you understand the message of the poem.

Conclusion ⑤

The questions raised by 'The Charge of the Light Brigade' are still relevant today. Wars are still being fought and orders are still being obeyed. Mistakes and misunderstandings are not unheard of and tragic consequences are turned into our daily news. '9/11' is a modern tragedy and we know the fate of those who were trapped by the flames. Both poems deal with conflict but the way they deal with deeper issues is very different. We are told to 'Honour the Light Brigade'; similarly we sympathise with the protagonist in 'Out of the Blue' who is "trying and trying", but his death is portrayed as bleak and desperate rather than honourable.

> Make sure your conclusion answers the question.

THIS IS A FLAP.
FOLD THIS PAGE OUT.

# The Controlled Assessment

I expect you'd find it helpful to know what <u>kind of questions</u> you're going to get asked, how best to <u>approach</u> them and what you'll be <u>marked</u> on.  So I've done a nice page about it for you.

## You'll Be Marked on Three Main Things

<u>Whatever</u> question you get, you'll get marks for doing these <u>three</u> things.

Keep them in mind when you're <u>planning</u> and <u>writing</u> your answer.

(1) Giving your own <u>thoughts</u> and <u>opinions</u> on the poems and supporting the points you make with <u>quotes</u> from the text.

(2) <u>Explaining</u> features like <u>form</u>, <u>structure</u> and <u>language</u>.

(3) Describing the <u>similarities</u> and <u>differences</u> between poems.

This means you should always <u>compare</u> the poems you're writing about.

## Here Are Some Example Questions

**EXAMPLE QUESTION 1**

Compare the different ways conflict is presented in a range of contemporary and Literary Heritage poems.

**EXAMPLE QUESTION 2**

Explore how the poems you have studied use structure and language to describe conflicts.

1)  You can <u>choose</u> which poems you write about, but you <u>must</u> include <u>at least</u> <u>one contemporary</u> and <u>one Literary Heritage</u> poem.  The number of poems you write about is <u>up to you</u>, but make sure you have <u>plenty to say</u> about each one.

2)  Even though the question doesn't specifically ask you to <u>compare</u> the poems, that's what you <u>have to do</u> to get good marks.

## Think About How You're Going to Tackle the Question

The question you get might be quite <u>general</u>, so you're going to have to think about the <u>best</u> <u>way</u> to approach it.  You might find it <u>helpful</u> to start off with a <u>basic plan</u> like the one below.

- Choose poems which relate to the <u>theme</u> of the question.
- Look at the <u>language</u> — what effect does it create?  <u>How</u> does it do this?
- Look at the <u>form and structure</u> — what effect do they create?  <u>How</u> do they do this?
- What are the <u>feelings and attitudes</u> in the poems?

How do the poems <u>compare</u> with each other?

## Prepare your answer carefully...

The question is set by your teacher, but you'll always be <u>marked</u> in the <u>same way</u>.  Always write about <u>language</u>, <u>form</u> and <u>structure</u>, as well as the <u>feelings and attitudes</u> in the poems.

# The Controlled Assessment

A <u>good plan</u> will help you organise your thoughts and write a <u>clear</u>, <u>well-structured</u> essay — which means lots of <u>lovely marks</u>. And the good news is, you'll have <u>plenty of time</u> to prepare one.

## Choose Your Poems <u>and</u> Map Out Ideas

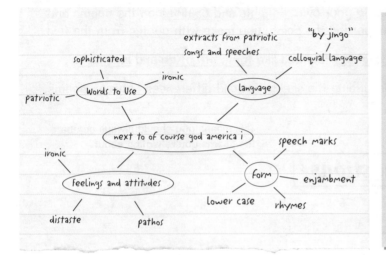

1) Let's say that for <u>Example Question 1</u> on page 65, you decide to write about <u>next to of course god america i</u>.

2) You might want to <u>map out</u> your <u>ideas</u> like on the left, so you can decide what to include in your detailed <u>plan</u>.

3) It's a good idea to do this for <u>all</u> your poems and make <u>links</u> between them.

4) Write down some <u>key quotes</u> you want to include in your essay too.

## Write a <u>Detailed</u> Plan

Here's an <u>example plan</u> for Question 1 on the last page. You can make it fairly <u>detailed</u>, as you've got enough time.

For some ideas on different ways to plan, see page 56.

Introduction
Key points of essay
Different presentations of conflict

Feelings and Attitudes
- Light Brigade — duty, honour
- Right Word — fear, compassion
- Flag — freedom, conscience
- next to of course — irony

Language
- Light Brigade — patriotic — "Noble six hundred"
- Right Word — uncertain, hesitant — "Is that the wrong description?"
- Flag — questioning, defining — "It's just a piece of cloth"
- next to of course — patriotic, ironic — "heroic happy dead"

Form and Structure
- Light Brigade — formal, drives forward, rhymes
- next to of course — hidden complexity, rhymes
- Right Word — short stanzas, punctuation
- Flag — rhetorical questions, rhymes, ends with rhyming couplet

Conclusion
- Different approaches for different purposes
- 'Light Brigade' works as a tribute, 'Flag' and 'next to of course' warn of the dangers of patriotism, 'Right Word' tries to avoid conflict

## Plan what you're going to write about before you start...

Use your preparation time <u>wisely</u> to come up with a <u>good plan</u> for your essay. You won't be allowed it with you when you're writing up, but you can have a <u>few notes</u> to jog your memory.

# The Controlled Assessment

Here are some grade 'A' paragraphs from a sample answer to Example Question 1 on page 65.

## Here's a Sample Introduction

Write an introduction that makes it clear you've understood the question, like this one:

> Poetry looks at all aspects of human life and the tragedies of conflict are an important theme in many poems. Each poet's insight and presentation of conflict is unique and coloured by circumstances and individual experience. Tennyson's 'The Charge of the Light Brigade' is unambiguous in its theme of the bravery of the soldiers, while 'next to of course god america i' has a more complex approach. Doubt and uncertainty lie at the heart of Imtiaz Dharker's 'The Right Word' and 'Flag' is clear in its support for the overriding importance of conscience.

← Tell the reader the names of the poems you're going to discuss.

## Here are Some Sample Paragraphs

You've got 2000 words to really explore the poems in depth. You don't have to write about every little bit of the poems — focus on writing about a few key elements in detail.

> 'The Right Word' is written in the first person, the 'I' who feels vulnerable and threatened. The poem begins with a statement of fact that is called into question by the first line of the second stanza. Doubt and uncertainty plague the narrator; she is apparently searching for a proper definition and she searches for an appropriate term to label the threatening person "lurking" outside. It is as though her thoughts and her certainty are interrupted by a voice advising caution, a voice of reason that refuses to jump to possibly dangerous conclusions: "Outside the door,/ lurking in the shadows,/ is a terrorist." At this point she stops to think and asks herself: "Is that the wrong description?" Several times she attempts to define to her own satisfaction the stranger on the other side of the door; her realisation that "No words can help me now" leads her to see that she must rely on her own humanity.

← Make it clear what each paragraph's about in the first line.

← Aim to develop your ideas.

← Analyse the language closely.

It's important to give your own opinions on the poems. Make your interpretations sound more convincing by giving plenty of evidence to support your argument — this means using lots of quotes.

> 'next to of course god america i' makes sophisticated use of extracts from patriotic songs and speeches in order to appear, at first glance, conventionally nationalistic. But this initial impression is soon demolished at a closer reading, as the poet links these sentiments with deaths caused by the resulting conflicts. Putting "god" and "america" in lower case letters suggests a lack of respect for patriotism, and at the end of the second line there are the throwaway words "and so forth". Any semblance of blind, steadfast patriotism is shown to be false. These techniques are skilfully employed to achieve an ironic impact clearly demonstrated in the line, "they did not stop to think they died instead". These words echo 'The Charge of the Light Brigade': "Theirs not to reason why, / Theirs but to do and die...", but Cummings' poem has a much more scathing tone than Tennyson's and leaves the reader in no doubt about the connection between patriotism and conflict.

← Keep focused on the theme of the question.

← Look at the poem's wider messages.

← Remember to compare the poems.

# How to Write an A* Answer

It's what you've all been waiting for: absolutely underline everything you need to know to write an utterly fantastic, knock-the-examiner's-socks-off, quite-frankly-blummin'-amazing A* answer. Phew. Better have a cuppa first.

## Know Your Texts In Depth

1) Make sure you know the poems really well — you need to be able to write about them in detail.

2) Don't just re-tell the story of the poem in your essay though — and don't try to write down absolutely everything you know about it.

3) Instead, carefully select key bits of the text and focus on writing about them in depth.

## Look Closely at Language

To get top marks, you need to pay close attention to the language used in the poems.

> Ted Hughes's 'Hawk Roosting' makes very heavy use of words that denote the self: 'I', 'my', 'me' and 'mine'. The claim that "I hold Creation in my foot" leaves the reader in no doubt that the hawk is utterly self-absorbed and completely confident in its supremacy. There is no room for disagreement or debate, and it is not interested in social niceties or mere words: "No arguments assert my right". This creature has the power of life and death over its prey. Hughes's savage imagery of "tearing off heads" vividly conveys the hawk's nature.

Analyse the effects of key quotes.

Use synonyms to help explain the poet's language.

Always develop your ideas.

## Give Alternative Interpretations

1) You need to show you're aware that poems can be interpreted in more than one way.

2) If the poem's a bit ambiguous, or you think that a particular line or phrase could have several different meanings, then say so.

> In 'Come on, Come Back', we sympathise with the predicament of "The girl soldier Vaudevue" who has been left barely alive: "Only her memory is dead for evermore." We have some facts to hand but there are many uncertainties and ambiguities. The presence of the "enemy" may be seen as a threat, but the fact he is "Whittling a shepherd's pipe" creates a pastoral and almost peaceful image. This could suggest that he is a sympathetic character.

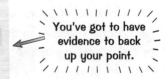
You've got to have evidence to back up your point.

3) Don't be afraid to be original with your ideas — you get marks for a personal response. Just make sure you can back up your arguments with plenty of evidence from the poem.

## Give some imaginative ideas...

You could gain marks for saying something a bit different, but you must be able to support your theories with quotes — otherwise you'll look like you don't know what you're talking about.

# How to Write an A* Answer

Even if your teachers aren't predicting you an A*, it's still <u>worth looking</u> at these pages to get a <u>few ideas</u> on how you could <u>improve</u> your work. This <u>quoting</u> lark for example — everyone should have a glance at that.

## Always Support Your Ideas with Details from the Text

This might seem like a fairly basic point — but if you don't <u>back up your ideas</u> with <u>quotes</u> or <u>references</u> from the text, then you're not going to get <u>top marks</u>. Here are some quoting <u>top tips</u>:

1) Choose your quotes <u>carefully</u> — they have to be <u>relevant</u> to the point you're making.

✓ The narrator in 'Out of the Blue' is pleading for attention: "Does anyone see / a soul worth saving." He is terrified and wonders if he is worthy of being rescued.

✗ The character in 'Out of the Blue' asks a powerful question: "So when will you come? / Do you think you are watching, watching a man shaking crumbs / or pegging out washing?"

This bit's not needed.

2) <u>Don't</u> quote <u>large chunks</u> of text — it's not necessary and it wastes time.

3) <u>Don't</u> reel off <u>long lists</u> of quotes without <u>explaining</u> them. Remember, quotes are there as <u>evidence</u> to support your argument.

✗ The second line in each stanza in Robert Minhinnick's 'The Yellow Palm' follows the repeated refrain of "As I made my way down Palestine Street" with "I watched a funeral pass", "I heard the call to prayer", "I met two blind beggars"; ordinary events in the life of the city.

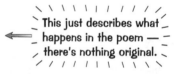 This just describes what happens in the poem — there's nothing original.

✓ In 'The Yellow Palm', scenes of ordinary city life are juxtaposed with the consequences of violent conflict. Looking in through "the door of the golden mosque", we see the faithful within but we are warned "there was blood on the walls." Images connecting the ordinary with the tragic run as a thread through the poem.

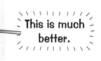 This is much better.

## Show Some Wider Knowledge

1) Do some <u>research</u> on the poems. Although you don't have to include <u>context</u>, it'll still look pretty <u>impressive</u>.

2) <u>Don't</u> go <u>overboard</u> though — your facts might be interesting, but you have to show they're <u>relevant</u> to your answer. It's best to keep your comments fairly <u>short</u>.

In Mametz Wood, Owen Sheers recalls "the wasted young" — the dead of the First World War (1914-1918) in which almost eight million soldiers lost their lives.

Tennyson's stirring poem recollects the fateful charge of the British 'Light Brigade' of cavalry; an incident that took place during the Battle of Balaklava in the Crimean War, when the Russians were defeated by the British and their French allies.

## Wider knowledge — sounds dangerous to me...

Quotes. Can't live with 'em, can't live without 'em as I believe the saying goes. Or a saying anyway. Think <u>carefully</u> about which ones to use and where, that's my advice. <u>Sorted</u>.

# How to Write an A* Answer

It's not just <u>what</u> you write that gets you an A* grade, it's <u>how</u> you write it.
Show some <u>finesse</u> with a <u>tip top vocabulary</u> and a lovely <u>flowing</u> writing <u>style</u>.

## Use Sophisticated Language

1) To put it simply, your writing has to sound <u>sophisticated</u> and <u>stylish</u>.

2) It should be <u>concise</u> and <u>accurate</u>, with no <u>vague words</u> or <u>waffle</u>.

3) It should also show off an <u>impressive range</u> of <u>vocabulary</u>.

4) Make sure it's <u>appropriate</u> though — <u>don't</u> use words if you don't
know what they really <u>mean</u>.

Style and sophistication are
Eddie's watchwords.

Not very sophisticated. ✗ Choman Hardi's narrator is a young child who doesn't get the adults' joy.

✓ The five-year-old narrator is a confused witness of the adults' happiness. ← This sounds much better.

This is too vague. ✗ Tennyson uses the same words a lot.

✓ Tennyson's use of repetition is highly effective. ← Use more specific language.

Don't keep using the same word to describe something. ✗ In 'Futility', the narrator shows that he feels sorry for the badly wounded soldier. He shows that he feels sorry for him when he asks for him to be moved "into the sun". The idea that he feels sorry is also shown towards the end of the poem.

✓ In 'Futility', the narrator expresses compassion for his dying comrade, asking that he be moved "into the sun". His sympathy and sense of loss is further expressed in the second stanza. ← Vary how you say things — it's far more interesting.

## Use Technical Terms Where Possible

At A* level, you need to use the <u>correct technical terms</u> when you're talking about poetry.
There's a handy <u>glossary</u> at the back of this guide that explains a lot of these terms for you.

<u>Don't write:</u>

✗ Ciaran Carson uses nice images

✗ The sentences run on from one line to the next...

✗ The poet uses touchy-feely words.

<u>Write:</u>

✓ Ciaran Carson uses effective metaphors

✓ The poet uses enjambment to...

✓ The poet uses emotive language...

## Think carefully about your choice of words...

You've got to sound like you <u>really know</u> what you're talking about — and the words you use to do
it will make a <u>big difference</u>. This kind of writing gets <u>a lot easier</u> with <u>practice</u> — so practise.

# How to Write an A* Answer

There's <u>more</u> to writing an <u>A* answer</u> than you thought, eh?  Still, we're <u>nearly done</u>.
This last page is a <u>real winner</u>, I'm sure you'll agree, so let's get cracking.

## Vary **Your** Sentence Structures

It's important to keep your reader <u>interested</u> in what you're saying.  One way to do
that is to vary the <u>style</u> and <u>length</u> of your sentences.  Look at these <u>examples</u>:

This is <u>boring</u> — it's dull and <u>repetitive</u>...

> Ciaran Carson's poem 'Belfast Confetti' uses a clever image to make his point.  He uses this clever image through the poem.  He uses it to round off the poem in its final two lines.  He calls the metal pieces of an exploding bomb a "fount of broken type".

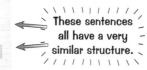
These sentences all have a very similar structure.

This is <u>varied</u> and much more <u>interesting</u>...

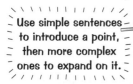
Use simple sentences to introduce a point, then more complex ones to expand on it.

> Belfast Confetti uses a sustained metaphor to convey its message.  Substituting "A fount of broken type" for the flying metal pieces of an exploding shrapnel bomb is an effective and thought-provoking poetic device.  At the end, the poet, in his confusion, is left with "A fusillade of question-marks."

## **Your** Writing **Should** Flow Around **Your** Quotes

To get an A*, your writing needs to <u>flow</u> beautifully.
This means working your quotes <u>seamlessly</u> into your sentences.

<u>For example</u>, instead of writing this...

> The main character in Armitage's 'Out of the Blue' is in mortal danger: "I am waving, waving", "Does anyone see / a soul worth saving", "The heat behind me is bullying, driving."

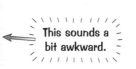
This sounds a bit awkward.

"Your writing should flow around your quotes like a river flows around stones."
CGP, 2010

...it's much <u>better</u> to write this:

> With his poignant, desperate plea, "So when will you come?", Simon Armitage's trapped protagonist, in despair and in hope, calls out to us all.

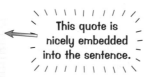
This quote is nicely embedded into the sentence.

## Proof-Read **Your** Work

1)  To get top marks, you need to avoid errors in <u>spelling</u>, <u>punctuation</u> and <u>grammar</u>.

2)  Once you've finished your work, spend time <u>checking</u> it over and <u>correcting</u> any <u>mistakes</u>.

3)  In the <u>exam</u>, leave yourself <u>five minutes</u> to read through your answer at the end.
    Put a <u>neat line</u> through any mistakes and write the correction <u>above</u>.

4)  In your <u>controlled assessment</u>, you're allowed more time and access to a dictionary or spell-check.
    This means your work will be marked much more <u>strictly</u> — so check it <u>carefully</u>.

## Leave time to prof-reed yuor work...

It might sound basic, but you seriously do need to <u>check your work</u> once you've finished.  It's easy
to make <u>silly mistakes</u> even if you're being really careful — and silly mistakes <u>don't look impressive</u>.

# Glossary

| | |
|---|---|
| adjective | A word that <u>describes</u> something, e.g. "big", "fast", "annoying". |
| alliteration | Where words that are close together <u>start</u> with the <u>same letter</u>. It's often used in poetry to give a nice pattern to a phrase. E.g. "<u>b</u>roken <u>b</u>ird's egg". |
| ambiguity | Where a word or phrase has <u>two or more</u> possible <u>meanings</u>. |
| assonance | When words share the same <u>vowel sound</u> but the consonants are different. E.g. "bl<u>o</u>cked with st<u>o</u>ps". |
| autobiographical | Describing something that happened in the <u>poet's life</u>. |
| ballad | A form of <u>poetry</u> that tells a <u>story</u> and often sounds quite <u>musical</u>. |
| blank verse | Poetry written in iambic pentameter that <u>doesn't rhyme</u>. |
| caesura | A <u>pause</u> in a line. E.g. Around the full stop in "The depth is appalling. Appalling". |
| colloquial | Sounding like everyday <u>spoken</u> language, e.g. "We grabbed a drink". |
| consonance | When words have the <u>same</u> consonant sounds but <u>different</u> vowel sounds, e.g. "t<u>a</u>ll / t<u>oi</u>l". |
| consonants | All the letters in the alphabet that <u>aren't vowels</u>. |
| contrast | When two things are described in a way which emphasises <u>how different</u> they are. E.g. A poet might contrast two different places or two different people. |
| dialect | A <u>variation</u> of a <u>language</u>. People from different places or backgrounds might use different words or sentence constructions. E.g. "by gum". |
| emotive | Something that makes you <u>feel</u> a particular <u>emotion</u>. |
| empathy | When someone feels like they <u>understand</u> what someone else is experiencing and how they <u>feel</u> about it. |
| end stopping | Finishing a line of poetry with the <u>end</u> of a <u>phrase or sentence</u>. |
| enjambment | When a sentence or phrase runs over from <u>one line</u> or <u>stanza</u> to the <u>next</u>. |
| first person | When someone writes about themselves, or a group which includes them, using words like "<u>I</u>", "<u>my</u>" and "<u>me</u>". |
| form | The <u>type</u> of poem, e.g. a sonnet or a ballad, and its <u>features</u>, like number of lines, rhyme, rhythm and meter. |
| free verse | Poetry that <u>doesn't rhyme</u> and has <u>no regular rhythm</u>. |
| iambic pentameter | Poetry with a <u>metre</u> of <u>ten syllables</u> — five of them stressed, and five unstressed. The <u>stress</u> falls on <u>every second syllable</u>, e.g. "They <u>fell</u>, like <u>snow</u>flakes <u>wip</u>ing <u>out</u> the <u>noon</u>". |
| iambic tetrameter | Like iambic pentameter but with a metre of <u>eight</u> syllables — four stressed and four unstressed. E.g. "O <u>what</u> made <u>fat</u>uous <u>sun</u>beams <u>toil</u>". |
| imagery | Language that creates a <u>picture in your mind</u>. It includes <u>metaphors</u> and <u>similes</u>. |
| internal rhyme | When two words in the <u>same line</u> rhyme. E.g. "Sitting <u>alone</u> on a round flat <u>stone</u> on a hummock there". |
| irony | When <u>words</u> are used in a <u>sarcastic</u> or <u>comic</u> way to <u>imply the opposite</u> of what they normally mean. It can also mean when there is a big difference between <u>what people expect</u> and <u>what actually happens</u>. |
| language | The <u>choice of words</u> used. Different kinds of language have <u>different effects</u>. |

# Glossary

| | |
|---|---|
| layout | The way a piece of poetry is visually presented to the reader, e.g. line length, whether the poem is broken up into different stanzas, whether lines create some kind of visual pattern. |
| metaphor | A way of describing something by saying that it is something else, to create a vivid image. E.g. "the china plate of a shoulder blade". |
| metre | The arrangement of stressed and unstressed syllables to create rhythm in a line of poetry. |
| monologue | One person speaking for a long period of time. |
| mood | The feel or atmosphere of a poem, e.g. humorous, threatening, eerie. |
| narrative | Writing that tells a story, e.g. the poem 'The Charge of the Light Brigade'. |
| narrator | The voice speaking the words that you're reading. E.g. 'At the Border, 1979' is written from the point of view of a young child, which means the young child is the poem's narrator. |
| oxymoron | A phrase which appears to contradict itself, because the words have meanings that don't seem to fit together, e.g. "heroic happy dead". |
| persona | A fictional character or identity adopted by a poet. Poets often create a persona so they can describe things from a different person's point of view, e.g. a male poet might use a female persona. |
| personification | A special kind of metaphor where you write about something as if it's a person with thoughts and feelings. E.g. "The kind old sun will know". |
| rhyme scheme | A pattern of rhyming words in a poem, e.g. in 'The Yellow Palm', the 2nd, 4th and 6th lines in each stanza rhyme. |
| rhyming couplet | A pair of rhyming lines that are next to each other, e.g. the last two lines of 'Flag'. |
| rhythm | A pattern of sounds created by the arrangement of stressed and unstressed syllables. |
| sibilance | Repetition of 's' and 'sh' sounds. |
| simile | A way of describing something by comparing it to something else, usually by using the words "like" or "as", e.g. "the world overflowing / like a treasure chest". |
| sonnet | A form of poem with fourteen lines, and usually following a clear rhyme scheme. There are different types of sonnets. They're often about love. |
| stanza | A group of lines in a poem. Stanzas can also be called verses. |
| structure | The order and arrangement of ideas and events in a piece of writing, e.g. how the poem begins, develops and ends. |
| syllable | A single unit of sound within a word. E.g. "All" has one syllable, "always" has two and "establishmentarianism" has nine. |
| symbolism | When an object stands for something else. E.g. A candle might be a symbol of hope, or a dying flower could symbolise the end of a relationship. |
| theme | An idea or topic that's important in a piece of writing. E.g. A poem could be based on the theme of war. |
| tone | The mood or feelings suggested by the way the narrator writes, e.g. confident, thoughtful. |
| voice | The personality narrating the poem. Poems are usually written either using the poet's voice, as if they're speaking to you directly, or the voice of a character. |
| vowels | The letters "a", "e", "i", "o" and "u". |

# Index

# *Index*

# <u>Acknowledgements</u>

The Publisher would like to thank:

**For poems:**

John Agard: 'Flag' — From *Half Caste and Other Poems* by John Agard, first published in the UK by Hodder Children's, an imprint of Hachette Children's Books, 338 Euston Road, London, NW1 3BH

Simon Armitage: Extract from *Out of the Blue* — Enitharmon, 2008, reproduced by permission of Enitharmon

Ciaran Carson: 'Belfast Confetti' — By kind permission of the author and The Gallery Press, Loughcrew, Oldcastle, County Meath, Ireland from Collected Poems (2008)

E.E. Cummings: 'next to of course god america i' is reprinted from *COMPLETE POEMS 1904-1962*, by E.E. Cummings, edited by George J. Firmage, by permission of W.W. Norton & Company. Copyright © 1991 by the Trustees for the E.E. Cummings Trust and George James Firmage.

Imtiaz Dharker: 'The Right Word' — Imtiaz Dharker, *The Terrorist at my Table* (Bloodaxe Books, 2006)

Choman Hardi: 'At the Border, 1979' — Choman Hardi, *Life for Us* (Bloodaxe Books, 2004)

Ted Hughes: 'Bayonet Charge' — From *The Hawk in the Rain*, 9780571086146, Faber and Faber, first published 1957

Ted Hughes: 'Hawk Roosting' — From Lupercal Faber and Faber; Reprint of 1970 edition (8 Oct 1985) ISBN-13: 978-0571092468

Robert Minhinnick: 'The Yellow Palm' — from *King Driftwood* (Carcanet, 2008) reproduced by permission of Carcanet Press Ltd

Margaret Postgate Cole: 'The Falling Leaves' — From *Scars Upon My Heart* selected by Catherine Reilly (Virago, 1981), reproduced by permission of David Higham Associates

Owen Sheers: 'Mametz Wood' — Copyright © 2005 Owen Sheers. Reproduced by permission of the author c/o Rogers, Coleridge & White Ltd., 20 Powis Mews, London W11 1JN

Stevie Smith: 'Come On, Come Back' — Estate of James MacGibbon

Jane Weir: 'Poppies' — By kind permission of Templar Poetry on behalf of the author, 2009

**For photographs:**

John Agard, Simon Armitage, E.E. Cummings, Ted Hughes, Robert Minhinnick, Owen Sheers — Rex Features
Ciaran Carson — Elzbieta Lempp / The Gallery Press
Imtiaz Dharker — Simon Powell
Choman Hardi — Bloodaxe Books
Wilfred Owen — Lebrecht Music and Arts Photo Library / Alamy
Stevie Smith — Mary Evans Picture Library / Robin Adler
Alfred Tennyson — Mary Evans Picture Library
Jane Weir — Templar Poetry

*Every effort has been made to locate copyright holders and obtain permission to reproduce poems and images. For those poems and images where it has been difficult to trace the originator of the work, we would be grateful for information. If any copyright holder would like us to make an amendment to the acknowledgements, please notify us and we will gladly update the book at the next reprint. Thank you.*